PRAISE FOR

The depth of Soul Survivor's experience in youth ministry is finally available for youth groups everywhere! Soul Survivor Encounter utilizes the gospel to energize your students, impassion your leaders and immerse your community in the values of service, relationship, worship, justice and evangelism. Don't miss out on this series of truly fantastic resources!

Josh McDowell
Speaker
Author, *Evidence That Demands a Verdict*

Soul Survivor is undoubtedly in the center of this generation's fresh wind of the Spirit. The message is clear and spiritually motivating. This material is wonderful.

Jim Burns
Founder and President, YouthBuilders

When a devotional starts with quotes from Bono, Avril Lavigne or Mel Gibson, something's up. In the case of Soul Survivor Encounter, that something is starting with youths' real lives, not with a religious subculture. A refreshing mix of classical theology with feet firmly planted in the neighborhood.

Sally Morgenthaler
Speaker
Founder, Sacramentis.com and Digital Glass Videos

There is no greater challenge facing us today than to engage emerging generations with the truths of the Scriptures, and Soul Survivor Encounter hits the bull's-eye in how to go about doing that.

Dan Kimball
Author, *The Emerging Church: Vintage Christianity for New Generations*
Pastor, Vintage Faith Church, Santa Cruz, California

Soul Survivor is a win-win resource. Youth leaders win with user-friendly resources that bring depth to their ministries. Students win with engaging discussion and reflection tools that help connect the dots between their faith and their life.

Kara Powell
Executive Director, Fuller Seminary Center
for Ministry to Youth and Their Families

From the start, Soul Survivor Encounter grabs you and doesn't let go. This new series of materials for students is grounded in the Bible, in touch with the world, full of activities and ideas; a truly interactive thrill for students and their youth leaders!

Darlene Zschech
Worship Leader

Soul Survivor Encounter hits kids where they are on several levels. It is culturally current, interactive, community building and solidly biblical. It brings God's Word right into the teenage world with personal stories, practical application and action steps. It moves from information to transformation and is hip without being flip. With journaling, projects and daily devotions, the Christian life becomes whole, rather than an isolated Sunday experience. Most of all Jesus, the eternal Son of God, is presented as the compelling Lord to be worshiped and a friend to share life with 24/7.

Don Williams, Ph.D.
Speaker
Author, *Twelve Steps with Jesus*

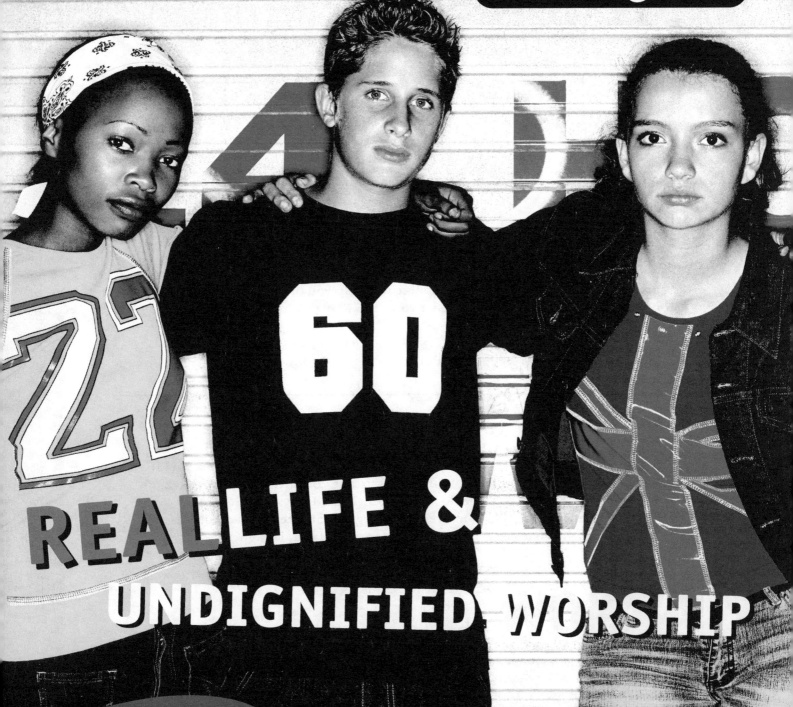

soul survivor
leader'sguide

60

REAL LIFE &
UNDIGNIFIED WORSHIP

soulsurvivor
encounter

Gospel Light
Mike Pilavachi, General Editor

Gospel Light

PUBLISHED BY GOSPEL LIGHT
VENTURA, CALIFORNIA, U.S.A.
PRINTED IN THE U.S.A.

Gospel Light is a Christian publisher dedicated to serving the local church. We believe God's vision for Gospel Light is to provide church leaders with biblical, user-friendly materials that will help them evangelize, disciple and minister to children, youth and families.

It is our prayer that this Gospel Light resource will help you discover biblical truth for your own life and help you minister to youth. May God richly bless you.

For a free catalog of resources from Gospel Light, please contact your Christian supplier or contact us at 1-800-4-GOSPEL *or* www.gospellight.com.

PUBLISHING STAFF
William T. Greig, Chairman • **Dr. Elmer L. Towns,** Senior Consulting Publisher • **Natalie Clark,** Product Line Manager • **Pam Weston,** Managing Editor • **Alex Field,** Associate Editor • **Jessie Minassian,** Editorial Assistant • **Bayard Taylor, M.Div.,** Senior Editor, Biblical and Theological Issues • **Mike Pilavachi,** General Editor • **Marcus Brotherton, Tom Stephen, Virginia Starkey,** Contributors • **Samantha Hsu,** Art Director • **Rosanne Moreland,** Designer

ISBN 0-8307-3531-3
© 2004 Gospel Light
All rights reserved.
Printed in the U.S.A.

contents

How to Use the Student Magazine

GETTING STARTED

All leader's notes, tips and activities that do not appear in the student magazine will appear in shaded areas. In completing the student magazine, you might have your students work on each session prior to a youth-group or small-group meeting, during which you can cover the material in more depth.

Every student magazine breaks down into sections that students can complete by themselves and in large or small groups. During your journey through the Soul Survivor Encounter, you and your students will find the following headings:

≡ status

Each session begins with quotations and interview excerpts under the Status heading. For more quotations and complete interviews, visit www.SoulSurvivorEncounter.com.

≡ the story

The Story contains the session's key issues. Students may also read a few verses from the Bible and hear stories that are key in understanding the session's topic.

≡ break it down

In Break It Down, students focus on the main points again by working on an individual creative project or activity.

≡ comeback

In Comeback, students meet in small groups to share thoughts on the topic and activities they completed in the Story and Break It Down sections.

≡ project revolution

The Project Revolution suggestions guide students in planning a project that they can do as a group or on their own. Their projects should be completed outside the church walls.

≡ momentum

This section challenges students to go deeper in Scripture. Check out Time in the Word—a five-day devotional. The Momentum section on the Soul Survivor Encounter website features further study options as well (see www.SoulSurvivorEncounter.com).

Ten years ago, Soul Survivor began in a little youth ministry at an Anglican church in a village called Chorleywood, outside of London. The heart of Soul Survivor is to encourage, equip, recruit, train and release young people into ministry.

I was an accountant until I was 29 years old; then God rescued me. He set me free and delivered me from the bondage of Egypt. One day the vicar of my Anglican church called me—he'd never done that before. He said, "Can you come and see me this evening?" And I thought, *Oh, my goodness, he's discovered some of my secret sins and I'm going to get rebuked*. I was really nervous, repenting and dealing with my issues.

I went to his house that evening, and to my relief, he hadn't discovered any of my secret sins. Instead, he wanted to give me the job as youth pastor. So I quickly said, "Yes," before he discovered my secret sins and changed his mind.

When I started as the youth pastor of this church, I wanted to be the best. I hit the ground running, organizing concerts, and young people from the whole area came out to see some of the best Christian bands in England, at least at that time.

You probably haven't heard of these bands because it was a generation ago. We had groups like Martin Joseph, Phil and John, and Fat and Frantic. There was actually a band called Fat and Frantic, and they were amazing. They actually wrote a song called "Last Night My Wife Hoovered My Head." I mean, it just says everything, doesn't it? It's wonderful.

Anyway, we filled the place with young people, and I thought, *Yes, I'm a success. Yes, look at all these young people*. But somewhere in the midst of that, I started to have this sinking feeling that all was not well. I realized that as more and more young people came to the gatherings and the events, our own youth group was shrinking. Then, after a couple of incidents, I realized that something was very wrong.

One night I decided to have a video evening. I got a film out and mounted these big TV monitors on the walls of the church lounge and hooked them up to a VCR. I blacked out the windows, and I bought—with my own money—popcorn, chips, peanuts and stuff like that. I put them in little bowls between the armchairs and got out sodas and drinks. I couldn't have done more if I had put on a frilly white dress and walked up and down the aisles during the intermission selling ice cream.

At the beginning of the evening the students arrived and sat down. I did a little stand-up comedy routine, and then we showed the main feature. As we did that, they had their popcorn, chips and peanuts, and they drank their sodas and drinks.

At the end of the evening, they all started to leave. As they walked out, I looked around, and I thought, *Oh, my goodness, this is a bomb site*. In this room, there were crushed peanuts, chips and popcorn on the carpet. There was even soda dripping from the walls and the tables. As I looked around, my heart sank. One of the last to leave was a girl named Emma, and she came up to me, folded her arms and said, "Mike, this room is a mess." And I thought, *Thank you for your discernment*. Then she said "You're going to have to get a Hoover to clean this," and she left. They all had left. They had left me to clean up their rubbish.

As I cleaned up their rubbish, I got more and more angry. As I vacuumed the carpet and washed the walls, I thought to myself, *These young people, they're not Christians. They're not disciples. They're consumers. All they ever do is take, take, take. They just consume everything. They don't have a disciple's bone in their bodies*. And I thought, *Right, from now on, every week, studies in Leviticus. I'll show them. That's the last time they get a band. That's the last time they get a video*.

I was so mad. Then, suddenly, in the midst of all that, this thought came into my mind: *And who made them like that?* You know what, I didn't need a sermon at that point because I knew that I'd made them like that. I'd made our relationship that of provider and client, and they'd done their job of being consumers brilliantly.

So I realized that I had a problem. By trying to entertain young people into the kingdom of God, I would have to spend the rest of my life entertaining them to keep them there. It wasn't working. Then I read this little book on how

Jesus discipled the disciples. I discovered that Jesus' method was very different from mine. I discovered how Jesus got beside them, and He did stuff with them and through them and then He sent them out.

There was a time when He sent them out in pairs to heal the sick and cast out demons. One time the disciples came across a boy possessed by a demon, but they couldn't cast it out. So they asked Jesus, "Oh, Lord, oh, Lord, why couldn't we cast out the demon?" And then Jesus said, and I'm going to paraphrase slightly here, "Well, good try, guys. It's good that you tried, but it didn't come out because you have too little faith" (see Matthew 17:19-20).

Now, after He said that, do you think they remembered that lesson? Do you think they remembered it better than if they'd gone to a daylong seminar on casting out demons and point *F* was, "This kind of demon comes out by faith?" I think they remembered that lesson because they had experienced failure.

Another time they came back, and they were like, "Oh, Lord, you should have been there. It was an amazing ministry trip! Even the demons flee when we tell them to leave in Your name" (see Luke 10:17).

And then Jesus said, "So you remembered the lesson about faith, huh?"

They probably replied, "Oh, yeah, faith—we remembered that."

Then He said, "Well done, guys, you sorted out that demon. I saw Satan fall like lightning from the sky and that suggests he didn't like what happened. But rejoice not that the demons flee; rejoice rather that your names are written in the book of life" (see Luke 10:18-20).

It was like He said, "You learned the faith lesson, now here's the next one: humility and the big picture." Jesus did that with them all the time.

That's how discipleship happens. We have to make space in our churches and in our ministries to allow people to mess up brilliantly. We need to devote ourselves to encouraging, affirming and reaching out to the next generation.

I long for us to seek Him for the next generation in so many different ways. To find ways of cheering them on so that they might be all they can be. To find ways of cheering them on so that they can be all they can be for the sake of the Lord and for the sake of the lost.

Mike Pilavachi
Ventura, CA
May 28, 2003

real life

Who Is God?

Note: All leader's options and tips are in shaded areas.

before everyone shows up

1. Pray for the students who will attend the meeting.
2. Gather materials needed to make name tags. Gather many different magazines, large index cards and a couple rolls of masking (or transparent) tape.
3. Work through the entire session on your own and mark the areas that you will focus on during the study. Ask God to give you creativity and a heart to listen to the Holy Spirit as you prepare.
4. **Optional Student Assignment:** Give students one week to complete this session on their own prior to coming to the meeting.
5. Keep your eyes and ears open for relevant celebrity quotations or news stories that could demonstrate the nature of God. You can add these as you go over the Status section. There are also more Status quotations and statistics available online at www.SoulSurvivorEncounter.com.
6. Gather materials for the study and make sure that all the technology that you will be using, such as a VCR or DVD player, works. Arrange seating so that everyone can see the screen or monitor.
7. View the corresponding Soul Survivor video segment ahead of time.
8. Play music and set out food to create a welcoming atmosphere.

GETTING STARTED

1. When students begin to arrive, greet everyone who enters the room and begin to learn names you don't already know.
2. Be sure to pray for God's guidance as you begin the study.

Icebreakers

Option 1: Prepare slips of papers with Bible verses to be read during the meeting. When the students arrive, give volunteers one passage to be read to the group. Be sensitive to those who may not like to read out loud.

Option 2: Instruct each student to grab an index card and then search through one of the magazines for pictures or phrases that describe aspects of his or her personality. Have students tape the pictures or words to the index cards and use them as name tags for the meeting.

Quoting Pop Culture
The goal of the Status quotations is to challenge students to hold each worldview up to the light of Scripture as they discover God's truth in each session.

Read through the quotations and the interview excerpt as a group. You will also want to discuss any other stories or quotations that you collected this week that might fit this week's topic, "Who Is God?" Invite students to comment as you read the quotes out loud.

> **Tip:** The Soul Survivor Encounter website is updated regularly with new quotations, interviews, icebreakers, video clips and more. Check it out today at www.SoulSurvivorEncounter.com.

WHAT PEOPLE ARE SAYING

MEL GIBSON, ACTOR

"Both my parents always had a tremendous amount of faith in God, even when times got rough and we were on welfare. They didn't give a hoot for money. My dad would say, 'It's a sin to worry. It's a lack of trust in God.'"[1]

BONO, LEAD SINGER, U2

"Judeo-Christianity is about the idea that God is interested in you—as opposed to *a god* is interested in you. This was a radical thought that God who created the universe might be interested in me. It is the most extraordinary thought" (emphasis added).[2]

THE DALAI LAMA

"To Buddhists, the idea of a Creator God sometimes sounds like nonsense. But these things don't matter; we can drop them. The point is that through these different traditions, a very negative person can be transformed into a good person. That is the purpose of religion."[3]

DAN HASELTINE, LEAD SINGER, JARS OF CLAY

Dan Haseltine, lead singer of the band Jars of Clay, wrote these words about the poverty in Africa: "Jesus Christ taught His followers that when they clothed the naked, they clothed Him. When they fed the hungry, they fed Him; when they visited the imprisoned, they visited Him. [But] the inverse was also true. If they ignored the downcast, they ignored Him."[4]

INTERVIEW

Subject: Gary Hale, student

Soul Survivor: What did you believe about God when you were younger?

Gary Hale: I believed in Him because I was told to, but I never looked for His work in my life. I went to church, but I never knew much about God or religion. When I was a junior in high school, a friend of mine invited me to her youth group. It was really fun, and I was scared because I thought people would think I was there just because my friends were there. They didn't judge me but just thought it was cool that I was there. So after that I started listening a little bit more.

See the rest of this interview and more thought-provoking quotes at www.SoulSurvivorEncounter.com.

After reading the quotes and the interview excerpt, ask students if they have heard any other stories or quotations during the week about the idea of exploring God.

Encourage students to keep their eyes and ears open during the coming week for what celebrities or friends might be saying about next week's theme, "Why We Need God."

video segment

Show the corresponding Soul Survivor video clip from *Real Life & Undignified Worship DVD.* Before students watch the video, hand out pieces of paper, pens or pencils. Ask them to write down what they feel as they hear what different folks believe about worshiping God.

Option: Show a clip from the movie *Simon Birch* (Buena Vista Home Entertainment, 1998). In one of the early scenes, Simon bursts out in church and gets reprimanded by the pastor. This scene can generate a great discussion on what God is really like.

the story

As you work through this section, you may want to have students read the different parts, or you may want to summarize the themes yourself. Let the Spirit give you guidance on how to best facilitate this section. You might share about a time from your own life when you saw a person you really wanted to meet and what happened.

One day at school, you see someone you have never seen before, who you totally want to get to know. What do you do?

You ask around, "You know that new person in our first period class? Do you know who she is?" To your amazement, it seems like everyone knows who she is and, at the same time, has a different opinion of her.

"Yeah, she's cute, but she thinks she's better than everyone else."

"Oh yeah, she's so nice!"

"I heard she came from the Midwest because her parents got divorced."

Now what do you do? All the people you talked to think they know this girl, but they all say completely different things about her. How do you find out what's true? You have to hang out with her, right? Spending time with someone is the best way to get to know that person.

The same is true with God. Everybody seems to have an opinion about God, but how do you find out the truth? You find out in the same way you would get to know a new person at school. You hang out with Him.

A LONG TIME AGO

Genesis, the first book in the Bible, literally means the beginnings. Genesis begins with two short stories about how God created everything.

In the first short story, chapter 1, God created everything in seven days. Literally, it's madness. God spoke into empty mist and things started appearing. And He has endless creativity. God made everything

from the duck-billed platypus to tulips to oceans and the Milky Way. God also made people. In this first story, God was awesome and sort of standoffish.

The second short story, chapter 2, also describes how God created everything, but this time we get the details. God shaped people out of the earth. And now, God was anything but standoffish when He dug in the dirt and breathed life into people. Talk about mouth-to-mouth resuscitation!

Action

Take a moment right now to read Genesis 1 and 2.

Read the two short stories (Genesis 1 and 2) together as a group. Be sure to take breaks and alternate readers and give students a chance to soak up the finer points of the story.

HANGING OUT WITH JESUS

Okay, so that's God in the beginning. But you have to admit that it seems hard to relate to a God who creates things on that scale. Such a creative God would construct a creative way to relate to His people, don't you think? After all, God hasn't come to my neighborhood and hung out in my room. Or has He?

Let's look at another book in the Bible that talks about how everything began. The book of John begins with these words:

> In the beginning was the Word, and the Word was with God, and the Word was God. He was with God in the beginning. Through him all things were made; without him nothing was made that has been made (John 1:1-3).

A little bit further it says, "The Word became flesh and made his dwelling among us" (John 1:14). One of the folks who translated and then paraphrased the Bible said it this way: "The Word became flesh and blood, and moved into the neighborhood" (John 1:14, *THE MESSAGE*). How cool is that? But what is "the Word"?

Well, the Word is Jesus (see John 1:10-14). So bottom line, John says that Jesus existed at creation (because Jesus is God), and Jesus came down into the neighborhood. Literally, God came to Earth so that we can fully know Him!

Action

Describe the difference God would make if He came into the world. Also, answer this question: Why would it be easier to relate to God if He became a man?

GETTING TO KNOW GOD

Think about a close friend of yours. Think about his or her personality, favorite clothes or the music he or she listens to. How long did it take you to discover these things about your friend? It probably took you more than just a few minutes, right?

Similarly, you must spend time with God to get to know Him. Jesus promised us that we could always be with God, because when Jesus left, He sent His Holy Spirit (see John 14:26-27). When people talk about the Trinity, this is what they mean. The Bible says that the one true God has always existed in three persons: God the Father; God the Son, Jesus; and God the Holy Spirit.

Now, check out this verse from a book of the Bible called Zephaniah:

> The LORD your God is with you, he is mighty to save. He will take great delight in you, he will quiet you with his love, he will rejoice over you with singing (Zephaniah 3:17).

Think about the line from Zephaniah, "He will quiet you with his love." This passage says that God wants to be your father. He wants to quiet the troubles of your life. Ask yourself, *How would God quiet me with His love if I let Him?*

Action

Look again at Zephaniah 3:17. Pick a phrase from the passage and write it down in the space provided. Look at the phrase and read it to yourself a few times. What does this phrase say about God? How does this phrase describe His relationship with you?

This would be a great time to play some meditative music in the background. Allow the music and the words of Scripture to radiate through the room.

⚡ break it down

If you have room, encourage students to find their own space to work on this section. As you do that, talk briefly about God's ability to make any space

sacred. Encourage them to find a sacred place where they can go each week during the Break It Down time.

Take a few minutes, read through the story and complete the activity.

ONE OF US

In March 1995, Joan Osborne released a single from her *Relish* album called "One of Us" that made everybody think about God as a human.

In the song, Osborne wonders if God is a regular person like the rest of us. She questions whether belief in God would mean believing in the God of the Bible. Is it possible that God could be like you and me?

We all want to relate to a God who understands what we're going through. Think about the Scripture passages we read that discuss the humanity of Jesus Christ (who is God), who visited our neighborhood.

Action

Create a list poem using a list of words and phrases that describe how you feel about God's having become a man and having stepped down into our neighborhood. What if God were sitting next to you or talking to you right now? Write down whatever words come to your mind when you think about that.

⚡ comeback

Have students form small groups of four to six to share their Break It Down poems and word lists, after which they can discuss the following questions.

Now get into groups and read your list poems to each other. If you are alone, find a friend or relative you can read your list poem to. Finally, discuss the following questions together:

- How can someone begin the quest of getting to know God?
- Why do you think God came down to Earth in the first place?
- Remember what Bono said about Christianity? What's so extraordinary about this idea? How is this different from other religions or philosophies?

project revolution

Keeping students in the same small groups, have them come up with a small project they will accomplish before they come back to next week's meeting. Remind them to complete this project outside the church walls. You may also want to talk briefly about how this project is a way of demonstrating integrity.

Write down your ideas for community-service projects that you can complete outside the church walls. Read the suggestions in this section to get you started.

BEING LIKE GOD

Our lives have changed because Jesus cared enough to spend time on Earth. Similarly, caring for someone in your life can have a massive impact. Think of someone who might benefit from your time this week: Is there a new kid in class you could eat lunch with? Do you have a sibling who's going through a rough time? Do you have a grandparent who needs help around the house? Does your neighborhood church have a ministry to seniors, a thrift store or a tutoring center? It takes only a little time to make a difference. Ask God, *Whom do You want me to serve with my time this week?* Then go for it!

RANDOM ACTS OF JESUS

Take an afternoon to walk around your community, meet people and act as you think Jesus would act. Ask yourself, *How would Jesus act if He met this person on the street?* Then go start meeting people. If you meet somebody, ask that person if he or she needs prayer for anything. Your prayer can be long or short, complicated or very simple. The important thing is to try to act more like Jesus.

When you get back, talk with your group (if you're in a group) about what you experienced, or write down your experiences (if you're alone) and share your thoughts with someone close to you.

 ## momentum

As the study comes to a close, remind students that if they want to go deeper this week there are many different ways to do that, including the Time in the Word Scripture readings. Also mention other options including the film, book and music recommendations on www.SoulSurvivorEncounter.com. Share what you will be doing during the week to go deeper in your own walk.

This devotional will help you start spending time with God regularly. You might want to keep a journal handy so that you can record your thoughts and reactions.

TIME IN THE WORD

Learn more about God by spending time reading His Word.

> **Day 1**—Colossians 1:15-20
> **Day 2**—Psalm 136
> **Day 3**—1 Corinthians 13
> **Day 4**—Isaiah 9:6
> **Day 5**—John 16:5-15

coming to a close

An important part of any small group is the time spent in prayer for one another. This is the group's time to hang out with God. This can be done in several ways.

1. Have students write out their specific prayer requests on an index card. These requests can be shared with the whole group, or students can pair up and trade requests with their prayer partner for the week.
2. Ahead of time, ask one student to close the session with prayer.

AFTER THE MEETING

1. **Evaluate:** Evaluate the meeting's overall effectiveness. Take time to talk to your volunteer leaders about how God worked, what went well, what did not go well and what needs to be changed before your next meeting.
2. **Encourage:** Try to contact each student during the week (phone calls, notes of encouragement, e-mail or instant messages), and welcome him or her to the group. Make yourself available to answer your students' questions.
3. **Equip:** Complete the next session on your own.
4. **Pray:** Prayerfully prepare for the next meeting.
5. **Project Revolution:** Complete your own project so that you can talk about it with your students.

Why We Need God

Note: All leader's options and tips are in shaded areas.

before everyone shows up

1. Complete your own Project Revolution activity as an example for the students.
2. Pray for the students who attended last week's study. As you pray, ask God to make you aware of what gets in the way of your own need for God. Perhaps God wants to use this study to help you find Him more fully.
3. Work through the entire session on your own and mark the areas you would like to spend more time on. As you prepare, ask God to give you creativity and the sensitivity to listen to Him.
4. Keep your eyes and ears open during the week for relevant celebrity quotations or news stories that demonstrate our need for God. You can also check the Status section at www.SoulSurvivor Encounter.com for more quotations.
5. Gather materials for the study and make sure that all the technology that you will be using, such as a VCR or DVD player, works. Arrange seating so that everyone can see the screen or monitor.
6. Play music and set out food to create a welcoming atmosphere.

GETTING STARTED

1. Have each small group share about their Project Revolution activity from last week.
2. Be sure to pray for God's guidance and grace as you begin the study.

Icebreakers

Option 1: Again, you may want to prepare slips of paper with Bible references to be read during the meeting. When students arrive, give volunteers one passage to be read to the group. Be sensitive to those who may not like to read out loud.

Option 2: Once all the students have arrived, ask them to introduce themselves to someone they haven't met before. Give all students two minutes to find out one interesting fact about the person they have just met that they can share with the whole group.

Before you read the quotations and the interview excerpt that follows, ask anyone if they saw something on TV or in a movie that demonstrated a need for God. Remind students to keep their eyes open for interesting stuff in the media.

WHAT PEOPLE ARE SAYING

HOMER SIMPSON, CARTOON CHARACTER

On an episode of the popular TV show *The Simpsons*, Homer says, "Oh, everything's too expensive these days. The Bible costs 15 bucks! And talk about a preachy book! Everybody's a sinner! Except this guy."

BEYONCÉ KNOWLES, SINGER

"God has a plan and God is in control of everything."[1]

STEVEN TYLER, LEAD SINGER, AEROSMITH

"You just don't want to get caught up doing [drugs] all the time, because then you lose the original force of creativity. I wrote a lot of songs high, [but] I wrote better ones sober."[2]

MIRANDA OTTO, ACTOR, LORD OF THE RINGS

"*Lord of the Rings* reveres and talks about things I think society is aching to go back to. A lot of films these days concentrate on so many negative aspects of society. In the '40s, [onscreen] ideals were about honor, loyalty and dignity—qualities that we tend to forego so quickly for money."[3]

LAYNE STALEY
FORMER LEAD SINGER, ALICE IN CHAINS

The former singer of Alice in Chains, Layne Staley, who was recently found dead, told *Rolling Stone* in 1996, "[Drugs] worked for me for years, and now they're turning against me—and now I'm walking through hell. I didn't want my fans to think that heroin was cool. But then I've had fans come up to me and give me the thumbs up, telling me they're high. That's exactly what I didn't want to happen."[4]

CLAY AIKEN, SINGER

"There are a lot of artists who may not be the best role models, the ones where parents are turning the radio down when their kids are in the car. I want to make sure that I'm setting a good example. It's something I'm aware of and actually proud of."[5]

INTERVIEW

Subject: Don Williams, speaker, author
Soul Survivor: How did you know that Jesus was real for you?
Don Williams: I went to a weekend Young Life camp in [California's] San Bernardino mountains, heard the gospel preached passionately by Jim Rayburn, the founder of Young Life, and opened my heart to Jesus. I knew that Jesus loved me, died for me and that if I chose to reject Him, I was saying, "Jesus, stay out of my life and stay on the cross." The next afternoon, [I] stood before 500 kids and verbalized that Jesus had come into [my] life. I knew Jesus was real and that He was (and is) in my life from that weekend to this moment [51 years later].

See the rest of this interview and more thought-provoking quotes at www.SoulSurvivorEncounter.com.

Also highlight one other story or comment you heard in the media during the past week that demonstrated our need for God. Finally, encourage students to keep their eyes and ears open during the coming week for quotations or stories about worship, which is next week's topic.

video segment

Show the corresponding Soul Survivor video clip from *Real Life & Undignified Worship DVD*. Before students watch the video, hand out pieces of paper and pens or pencils. Ask them to write down what they feel as they hear what different folks believe about worshiping God.

Option: Show a clip from The Simpsons episode titled "Homer the Heretic." In this episode Homer stops going to church and experiences some short-term benefits (i.e., being able to go to the bathroom with the door open). Ask the question, How does Homer's attitude exemplify how many people feel about the Church and God?

≣ the story

Do you ever feel like the world is a tough place to live or that life isn't the way it should be?

When things go wrong—your parents get divorced, friends commit suicide or when people are downright evil toward one another—all of us have this sense that things are somehow supposed to be different.

WHERE IT ALL BEGAN

When God finished creating the world on the seventh day, He proclaimed everything to be very good. Adam and Eve lived in paradise and they felt no shame (see Genesis 2:25). Do you suppose they lived happily ever after? No, because this story is not a fairy tale, and something changed their lives (and ours) forever.

I don't know what paradise would look like for you, but for Adam and Eve paradise consisted of all the food they wanted, no boring work, walking around naked and plenty of time to "fill the earth" (Genesis 1:28).

God gave them one rule to follow. God said, "You are free to eat from any tree in the garden; but you must not eat from the tree of the knowledge of good and evil, for when you eat of it you will surely die" (Genesis 2:16-17). No problem, right? Wrong.

When a server at a restaurant says, "Be careful, the plate is hot," what do most people do? Most people touch the plate to make sure. Our *free will* gives us the freedom to do good stuff and, equally, the stupid stuff too.

Adam and Eve had free will too. Guess what happened when God told them not to eat the fruit of this particular tree?

One day, as the couple stood near the tree, the serpent (aka Satan) told the woman that if she ate the fruit she would become like God (see Genesis 3:4). So she ate the fruit. Adam followed her example, and all of a sudden, things weren't the way they were supposed to be. They both realized they were naked and freaked out, hiding from each other and from God (see Genesis 3:8).

WHAT ABOUT JESUS?

Do you believe in capital punishment (i.e., the death penalty)?

What if someone killed your best friend? Would he or she deserve death? Most of us, if questioned long enough, could think of a situation that would justify the death penalty. What about people who are caught cheating on their spouse, should they be put to death?

In Jesus' day, the law said that a woman caught cheating on her husband should be stoned to death (no drugs here, real stones). A group of people would throw large rocks at her until she was dead.

Action

Read about how Jesus dealt with a situation involving adultery in John 7:53—8:11.

GOD'S CREATIVE WORK CONTINUES

In the passage you just read, Jesus reminded the crowd of a basic truth: Everybody sins. Since that episode in paradise, everyone has been separated from God because of sin.

That's why you don't always do what's right, even though you know the difference between right and wrong. That's why your friends and family let you down sometimes. These things happen because our sin separates us from God.

So how can we make things right and enter into a close relationship with God? We need to listen to Jesus' words from the story in John: "Then neither do I condemn you, . . . Go now and leave your life of sin" (8:11). God established a relationship with Adam and Eve after their sin. Even today, God wants to establish a relationship with everyone.

Jesus grew up and lived a perfect life on Earth, showing us how to live. Then He died for us so that we wouldn't have to pay the eternal consequences for our sins. We can't return to the Garden of Eden, but we can still walk closely with God every day of our lives.

God offers you life right now. Being with God may be totally new to you, or you may be coming back to a relationship that began a long time ago. Either way, a relationship with God begins with a prayer.

Action

Write the word "sin" in the middle of a sheet of paper. Around the word "sin," write words or draw pictures of what that sin looks like in your life.

Demonstrate how to do this by writing some of your own sins on a piece of paper. Emphasize, however, the importance of being personal and honest with God. Remind the students that it is okay if they do not want to share their sins with the group.

PRAYER

Talk to God right now about being in a closer relationship with Him. Thank Him for sending His Son so that you can have eternal life. Ask Him to forgive your sins. Ask the Holy Spirit to help you serve God completely. Write down all your thoughts and feelings after you pray.

Give students time to journal. After they have spent some time alone with God, let them know that you will answer any questions they may have about a relationship with Jesus Christ, especially if some students have never made this commitment. Also, talk briefly about your own experience of making a commitment or recommitment to Christ.

≦ break it down

Remind students that this is their private time with God. Remind them about the importance of sacred space. If they found a spot last week, encourage them to go back to the same spot and ask God to make that space sacred or to set it apart for their time with Him.

> REMINDER: Be sure that you take time to find a sacred space as well. This is time for you to pray for the students and to pray about how God wants to use the rest of your time together.

As you begin this section, take time to pray for people you know who need to experience God's love and forgiveness. You may need to forgive someone in your own life. Tell God about it now.

GOD'S AMAZING LOVE

John Newton bought and sold people. He kidnapped people in Africa and then sold them as slaves. He drank a lot because of the guilt he felt in doing this.

One day, everything changed. Newton faced the intense error of his ways and heard God's words that he was not condemned and that he should leave his life of sin. He expressed his joy by writing the classic hymn "Amazing Grace."

Action

Take a few minutes to write down your thoughts in the space provided. Write down your feelings about grace. Write about your need for God, and if you feel like it, write your thoughts and feelings in the form of a story, a poem or a song.

Option: Invite several volunteers to read their stories, poems or songs to the entire group. Obviously, they shouldn't be forced to read if they don't feel like it.

≦ comeback

Have your students form small groups. After the small groups have shared their Break It Down stories, poems and songs, ask each small group to answer the Comeback questions. If they finish early, remind them to start thinking through what project they plan to complete this coming week.

Now get into small groups and discuss your stories, poems and/or songs. Share some of the things you've written down and then discuss the following questions together:

- Why do you think so many people haven't heard the good news about Jesus and God's love if what the Bible says is true?
- Are Christians doing a bad job of sharing their faith, or are people just not listening?
- Define the word "grace" together. Why is God's grace so important, so amazing?

⚡ project revolution

Let's translate your thoughts into action. With your group, brainstorm several ways to serve your local community. Read the suggestions in this section to get you started.

ENCOURAGE A MISSIONARY

How can you make a difference in the world for those outside your church walls? Find a missionary for whom you could pray regularly. Send that missionary (or group of missionaries) notes of encouragement, letters or a care package. You may also find someone who makes a difference in your own community and serve that person by sending him or her a letter or gift or by volunteering your own time.

GOING BACK TO EDEN

In the Garden of Eden, Adam and Eve walked around naked but unashamed. God created us to look inside people, not at the exterior of their lives. Sometime this week, go to your downtown area and meet someone who is homeless or stricken by poverty. Maybe your group could offer to buy that person a cup of coffee or a meal—or just talk with him or her. Live out what it means to see the inside of people and not be turned off by what's on the outside. **Note:** Bring someone with you if you decide not to complete this project as a group.

⚡ momentum

Do you feel God calling you to go deeper in understanding your need for Him? Check out the Scriptures in Time in the Word.

TIME IN THE WORD

Thinking about sin isn't fun but you will discover great joy when you're honest before God. Each day, read the passage and record your thoughts in a journal.

Day 1—2 Samuel 11:2-15
Day 2—Psalm 51
Day 3—Romans 3:23-26
Day 4—1 John 1:5-10
Day 5—Romans 8:1-2

review

Soul Survivor, by Mike Pilavachi (Regal Books, 2004)
Review by Alex Field

Mike Pilavachi's book *Soul Survivor* is a manifesto written for people who feel like they're stranded in a desert far from God. Over the course of 11 chapters, Pilavachi explains how God can sometimes work even more powerfully in the dry times of our lives—because the desert forces all of us to seek after God even more intensely. Pilavachi, who mentored worship leaders Matt Redman and Tim Hughes, describes the desert as a crucible in which the waste is burned away to produce character and humility.

In his own striking and humorous prose, Pilavachi captures the essence of both the valley and the mountaintop, saying that without the one the other has less meaning. The book is a marvelous way to refocus your eyes on what's important in life, so you don't miss out on the work God might be doing.

In *Soul Survivor*, Pilavachi instructs, "Don't settle for a superficial version of Christianity. Superficial Christianity is the most boring thing in the world. Go for broke! Ask your Lord to take you deeper. Don't be satisfied any longer to exist in security; choose to live in adventure. Say yes to His plans for you, and as He begins to unfold them, stay there. Don't run away. Then you will come up from the desert, leaning on your lover, ready to be a voice and not another echo, equipped to change the world."[6]

coming to a close

1. Have the group come back together for prayer. Students can either pray with their prayer partners or pray together as a group. Be sure to have

index cards available so that the students can write down their prayer requests and then trade them with their prayer partners.

2. If possible, soften the lights and light a candle before the group moves into prayer. Allow the silence and the candle to help center the group.

3. Explain that if anyone wants to talk more about a relationship with Jesus Christ, you would love to talk with him or her. Also, be sensitive that some might feel the need to address a specific sin. Pray for God to give you wisdom and sensitivity to care for the group.

AFTER THE MEETING

1. **Evaluate:** Discuss what went well and what did not go well.
2. **Encourage:** If you have a large group, divide the list of students among the adult leaders in order to make personal contact with each student this week.
3. **Equip:** Complete the next study.
4. **Pray:** Prayerfully prepare for the next meeting.
5. **Project Revolution:** Complete your own project.

A Lifestyle of Worship

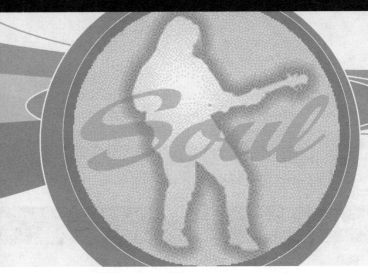

Note: All leader's options and tips are in shaded areas.

before everyone shows up

1. Pray for all the students who will attend and the friends they may invite.
2. Complete your own Project Revolution commitment from last week.
3. If you are able, gather pictures of different ways that people worship and put them up around the room.
4. Work through the entire session on your own and mark the different areas where you would like to spend the most time during the study. As you prepare, ask God to give you creativity and a heart to listen to Him.
5. Keep your eyes and ears open during the week for relevant quotations or news stories that would demonstrate how people worship.
6. Gather materials for the study and make sure that all the technology that you will be using, such as a VCR or DVD player, works. Arrange seating so that everyone can see the screen or monitor.
7. View the corresponding Soul Survivor video segment ahead of time.
8. Play music and set out food to create a welcoming atmosphere.

≋ status

Before you read the quotations and the interview excerpt, ask students if they saw or heard anything in the media during the past week that had to do with worship.

WHAT PEOPLE ARE SAYING

SHARON STONE, ACTOR

Sharon Stone told *USA Today* about her brush with a brain aneurysm: "It was a very painful journey to have that, and it's been a long arduous journey back. There's that old-time kind of gospel song called 'A Closer Walk with Thee.' I think that's what the walk back has brought me. It's been a very peaceful and lovely thing."[1]

PAUL McCARTNEY, MUSICIAN

"I have such an admiration for John [Lennon], like most people. But to be the guy who wrote with him, well that's enough. Right there you could retire and go, 'Jesus, I had a fantastic life. Take me, Lord.'"[2]

BOB DYLAN, MUSICIAN

"You hear a lot about God these days: God, the beneficent; God, the all-great; God, the Almighty; God, the most powerful; God, the giver of life; God, the creator of death. I mean, we're hearing about God all the time, so we better learn how to deal with it."[3]

AFROMAN, RAPPER

"I'm just changing my topic. I've told people about a whole lot of bad stuff—why not throw in some good stuff? I may be a Christian now, but I can still rap."[4]

INTERVIEW

Subject: Matt Brookes, worship leader at Ventura Vineyard Church

Soul Survivor: Years ago you got in a car accident that resulted in a broken arm and broken legs. Did the accident impact your relationship with God?

Matt Brookes: This is when I found a call to worship. I mean real worship. I spent a lot of time alone with God worshiping because I couldn't do anything but play guitar. Up until then I was at the stage where leading worship was merely singing and playing songs I liked. I wasn't focused on the content or the words in general. I began to realize that worship is singing *to* God. It is not just melody lines; they are prayers.

See the rest of this interview and more thought-provoking quotes at www.SoulSurvivorEncounter.com.

Remind the group to keep their eyes and ears open for interesting things in the media for next week, when the session will explore trusting God, or faith.

video segment

Show the corresponding Soul Survivor video clip from *Real Life & Undignified Worship DVD*. Before students watch the video, hand out pieces of paper and pens or pencils. Ask them to write down what they feel as they hear what different folks believe about worshiping God.

Option: Show a clip from the movie *Keeping the Faith* (Touchstone Pictures, 2000) in which the Rabbi (played by Ben Stiller) brings in a gospel choir for worship in his synagogue. This scene and the discussion that follows can create a fruitful discussion about worship.

≋ the story

Huge? Yeah, God's huge.
WARNING! DANGER! STOP! You are in danger of missing the point!

Action

Stop reading this study. Stop journaling. Stop everything and go outside. Listen and be still. Quietly study the sky. Let the Holy Spirit speak to your soul as you notice God's creation. Come back inside after five minutes.

Ask the group to see this time outside as an opportunity to learn. Experiencing God in His creation is another way to fully understand why we worship. If going outside isn't an option, show pictures of the universe or ask students to simply close their eyes and imagine a time when they saw the incredible vastness of the universe.

THE WONDER OF IT ALL

Read this poem written by a guy who spent a lot of time looking up at the sky:

> O LORD, our Lord, how majestic is your name in all the earth! When I consider your heavens, the work of your fingers, the moon and the stars, which you have set in place, what is man that you are mindful of him, the son of man that you care for him? (Psalm 8:1,3-4).

Do you ever feel tiny compared to the universe? A man named David wrote this worship song. David became a great king of Israel, but when he was younger he was a shepherd who worshiped God under a vast sky of stars.

David knew he was small compared to God. David also knew that God cared for him personally, despite His massive power. This caused David to worship. Think about that idea for a second. How does that make you feel?

DOES WORSHIP STOP WHEN THE MUSIC STOPS?

Anna bought Tom a rose to show him that she loved him. She put the rose on his desk with a note that read, "Anna." When Anna saw Tom the next day, he didn't mention the rose. She worried that he didn't love her, so she asked him about it. "Oh, thanks for the rose; I gave it to my mom. She loves flowers," Tom replied. Anna had hoped for a different response. What went wrong?

Anna didn't know Tom's love language. Some people like gifts; some like hugs; others appreciate compliments. Everyone's love language is a little bit different. Anna wanted to show her love, so she gave Tom what she would have wanted to receive as a gift.

Pause here to be sure that students understand the idea of love languages—how different people feel loved in different ways, including gifts, compliments, physical touch and others. You may want to share an example from your life of a time when someone understood your language of love or a time when someone did not.

Does God have a love language? Sometimes we experience the greatness of God's love and feel like expressing our gratitude, but we struggle to find the words. We know God loves to hear us praise Him, but He desires so much more.

> Therefore, I urge you, brothers, in view of God's mercy, to offer your bodies as living sacrifices, holy and pleasing to God—this is your spiritual act of worship (Romans 12:1).

What is God's love language?

God loves it when we present to Him *everything* in our lives, including our time, money, relationships and even our ability to serve others. We worship God when we give Him the whole of our lives.

Action

Reflect on Romans 12:1. In the space provided, jot down an answer to the question following each phrase.

> *"Therefore, I urge you, brothers, in view of God's mercy."*
> How have you experienced God's mercy in your life or seen it in the lives of others?

> *"Offer your bodies as living sacrifices, holy and pleasing to God."*
> In what ways have you sacrificed your life or seen others sacrifice their lives to God in worship or service?

> *"This is your spiritual act of worship."*
> How do you think the world would respond if Christians worshiped God by serving others?

JESUS, WORSHIP LEADER

Jesus told a story about the entire world coming together for the final worship service in heaven. At this massive event, the King tells His people what He valued about the lives they led.

> Then the King will say to those on his right, "Come, you who are blessed by my Father; take your inheritance, the kingdom prepared

for you since the creation of the world. For I was hungry and you gave me something to eat, I was thirsty and you gave me something to drink, I was a stranger and you invited me in, I needed clothes and you clothed me, I was sick and you looked after me, I was in prison and you came to visit me." Then the righteous will answer him, "Lord, when did we see you hungry and feed you, or thirsty and give you something to drink? When did we see you a stranger and invite you in, or needing clothes and clothe you? When did we see you sick or in prison and go to visit you?" The King will reply, "I tell you the truth, whatever you did for one of the least of these brothers of mine, you did for me" (Matthew 25:34-40).

Caring for the needy *is* an act of worship. When you meet the needs of the poor, the hungry, the homeless or the naked, you speak Jesus' love language—in fact, you are actually serving Jesus Himself.

≋ break it down

Complete the Break It Down section individually.

ALTERNATIVE WORSHIP

C. S. Lewis and Mother Teresa both loved God and worshiped Him in radical ways. Check out what these radical worshipers have to say about worship.

C. S. Lewis

"I think we delight to praise what we enjoy because praise not merely expresses but completes the enjoyment. It is not out of compliment that lovers keep on telling one another how beautiful they are, the delight is incomplete till it is expressed."[5]

Mother Teresa

An interviewer asked Mother Teresa, "Do you find it easy to carry out your work among the poor?" She responded:

> Of course it would not be easy without an intense life of prayer and a spirit of sacrifice. It wouldn't be easy either if we didn't see the poor—Christ—who continue to suffer the sorrows of His passion. At times, we would be happy if we could get the poor to live peacefully with each other. It is so hard for those who have been deprived of their basic needs to live in harmony and support their neighbors, and not see them as dangerous competitors, capable of making their state of misery even worse! That's why we cannot offer them anything but our testimony of love, seeing Christ Himself in each one of them, no matter how repugnant they seem to us.[6]

Action

Choose one of these quotations and respond to it. What feelings do you have when you read the quotation? How do the words affect your view of worship? Now write your own worship statement—write what worship is to you in your everyday life.

≋ comeback

Now get into small groups and read your worship statements. If you are alone, read your statement to someone close to you. Then answer the following questions together:

- What does it mean to have a lifestyle of worship?
- How did Mother Teresa worship God by serving the poor?

project revolution

As students decide on a project, remind them that the purpose of this section is to try to take their faith outside the church. As the study continues, it is okay to do similar projects every week or to build on the same project. These suggestions are simply ways to help them think outside the box. Remember to decide on your own project and follow through as an example to the whole group.

Write down your ideas for local projects that you can do on your own or with your group. The suggestion in this section is here to help you get started.

THE R.A.W. DEAL

Practice a Radical Act of Worship (R.A.W.) one day this week. As a group, choose a worship song that each of you will think about for a 24-hour period. Read the lyrics of the song together. On the day you choose, take some time in the morning to meditate on the words of the song. At breakfast, read through the song lyrics again. While you're at school or work, keep the song lyrics in your pocket so that you can refer to them throughout the day. At lunch and dinner, read through the song again and think about the application of the song in your life. At the end of the day, write down how God used the song to give you a new perspective during the day. Share the results with your group.

momentum

As the study comes to a close, remind students of the different ways they can go deeper.

Do you want to go even deeper in understanding God's heart when it comes to worship? Read the Time in the Word verses this week.

TIME IN THE WORD

Spend time in God's worship book, Psalms, this week.

Day 1—Psalm 100
Day 2—Psalm 103
Day 3—Psalm 40
Day 4—Psalm 9
Day 5—Psalm 139

coming to a close

1. This week, end the meeting with a time of worship. You may want worship to be the closing prayer. After singing a couple of songs, instruct the group to leave in silence.
2. Another option, is to have the group pray as they have in previous weeks. Again, they can either pray with a partner or together as a group. Be sure to have index cards available for students to write down their prayer requests.

AFTER THE MEETING

1. **Evaluate**
2. **Encourage**
3. **Equip**
4. **Pray**
5. **Project Revolution**

Note: All leader's options and tips are in shaded areas.

before everyone shows up

1. Pray for each student individually and for the friends the students may invite.
2. Complete your own Project Revolution commitment from the previous week.
3. If possible, collect and display pictures of different famous people that have demonstrated a trusting walk with God; for example, Mother Teresa, Brother Andrew, Martin Luther King, Jr., etc.
4. If it has been helpful, continue to write out the Scripture verses ahead of time so that you can have people prepared to read them during the study. As always, be sensitive to those who do not like to read out loud.
5. Keep your eyes and ears open during the week for celebrity quotations or interesting stories that would demonstrate faith, or a trust in God, for the Status section.
6. Work through the entire session on your own ahead of time. Highlight the areas that you would like to spend more time with during the study. As you work through each section, picture the students and ask God to speak to them during the session.
7. Gather materials for the study and make sure that all the technology that you will be using, such as a VCR or DVD player, works. Arrange seating so that everyone can see the screen or monitor.
8. View the corresponding Soul Survivor video segment ahead of time.
9. Play music and set out food to create a welcoming atmosphere.

GETTING STARTED

1. When students arrive, check in with as many as possible and see how their week went.
2. Pray for God's guidance and grace as you begin the study.

Icebreakers

Option 1: Ask each person to share the hardest thing about the Project Revolution activities. You may even want to write on the board, "What makes it hard to do what God wants us to do?" Allow students to share freely, and create an atmosphere of open, honest communication.

Option 2: Ask students to talk about the person they respect the most in terms of living out their faith.

Ask the students if they noticed anything this week having to do with trusting God, or faith. Let them know that next week you'll be studying how to share your faith and ask them to keep their eyes and ears open to good and bad examples of people who have talked about or demonstrated their faith to others.

As you read, invite students to make comments or ask questions whenever they want.

WHAT PEOPLE ARE SAYING

AXL ROSE, LEAD SINGER, GUNS 'N' ROSES

Rose gave advice to fans waiting for a new Guns 'N' Roses album. "If you are waiting, don't. Live your life. That's your responsibility, not mine. But if you're really into waiting, try holding your breath for Jesus because I hear the payoff may be much greater."[1]

COLIN POWELL, SECRETARY OF STATE

"We must not listen to the siren songs of the bigots, extremists who cloak themselves in false spirituality in an attempt to divide and weaken us."[2]

KIRSTEN DUNST, ACTOR

"I think a lot of people are losing their religion. Definitely. Even me, I know that when I grew up, I used to go to church every Sunday, and now it's become holidays. But I think as long as you have your own thing, whether it's meditation—anything that centers you in life is good. Do I pray? Yeah, I do."[3]

ORLANDO BLOOM, ACTOR

"I try to maintain a sense of reality, and that comes from being with my friends and family. I try to stay real, to find the humanity in every character I play."[4]

INTERVIEW

Subject: Pete Hughes, Soul Survivor leader
Pete Hughes leads Soul Survivor's event team, most recently pulling off the massive Soul in the City mission that took place in London in August 2004.
Soul Survivor: When did you first meet God and understand His love for you?

Pete Hughes: I grew up knowing about God and His love for me from a very early age. However, when I was about 11, I suddenly became aware that I could know God more than just in an academic way, but actually in an intimate way. I realized that God loved me, not because of what I've done or what I could do, but because He's a perfect Father who loves His children perfectly. All the truths that I'd learned from childhood suddenly became real and moved from my head to my heart. It was at that conference that I responded to live my life for God.

See the rest of this interview and more thought-provoking quotes at www.SoulSurvivorEncounter.com.

video segment

Show the corresponding Soul Survivor video clip from *Real Life & Undignified Worship DVD*. Before students watch the video, hand out pieces of paper and pens or pencils. Ask them to write down what they feel as they hear what different folks believe about worshiping God.

Option: Show one of the final scenes from the movie *Bruce Almighty* (Universal Studios, 2003) in which Bruce (played by Jim Carrey) is praying to God on the side of a highway. Talk about what Bruce's character reveals about faith in his prayer.

the story

Ask your students if they think people today still suffer for what they believe. Research some areas of the world where Christians are put to death because of their faith and share a few examples. You may also briefly share about how you have experienced hard times because of your faith in Jesus Christ.

TO BE OR NOT TO BE

Read the following ancient text that describes how Nero treated Christians:

> First, then, the confessed members of the sect were arrested; next, on their disclosures, vast numbers were convicted, not so much on the count of arson as for hatred of the human race. And derision accompanied their end: they were covered with wild beasts' skins and torn to death by dogs; or they were fas-

tened on crosses, and, when daylight failed, were burned to serve as lamps by night. Nero had offered his gardens for the spectacle, and gave an exhibition in his circus.[5]

Have you ever attended a party at which the hosts burned people on crosses to light the way to the food and drink table? Christians of the first century lived out a radical faith. They risked their lives to follow Jesus, literally! Check out what Jesus says about those who follow him.

> Whoever wants to become great among you must be your servant, and whoever wants to be first must be your slave (Matthew 20:26-27).

> If anyone would come after me, he must deny himself and take up his cross and follow me. For whoever wants to save his life will lose it, but whoever loses his life for me will find it (Matthew 16:24-25).

THE INS AND OUTS OF FAITH

One of the earliest Christian churches experienced a laborious time in their history. People persecuted the church members for following Jesus, and they lost their faith after being one of the most passionate, outspoken churches around. This church received a letter that we call Hebrews. God knew this church needed a reminder of what faith is. Check out this definition of faith from Hebrews:

> Now faith is being sure of what we hope for and certain of what we do not see. And without faith it is impossible to please God, because anyone who comes to him must believe that he exists and that he rewards those who earnestly seek him (Hebrews 11:1,6).

So what is faith?

Let students discuss this question before going on. Talk about how different people understand faith differently. Remind them that during this study they will understand more about what the Bible means when it talks about faith.

Faith is having an inner confidence and trust that God will do what He promises. Faith is belief in God and acting on that belief.

Faith shows itself in many ways. For example, faith's *inward reality* shows itself when you pray for your friends, teachers or family members, trusting God to take care of them rather than worrying about them. Faith's *outward reality* shows up when you care for the needs of those friends and family members.

FOUR FAITHFUL FRIENDS

Jesus kept a full schedule. Mobs of people followed Him around hoping to see a miracle or get some free food. One day, when He visited His hometown, the house He was staying in was packed. People stood two or three deep outside the door. Four guys showed up carrying their buddy who couldn't walk. They believed that if Jesus could touch their friend, he would walk again.

Of course, they had a problem: They couldn't get into the house. So, what did their faith compel them to do? They climbed on the roof, dug a hole in the ceiling (the roof was a mixture of dirt, sticks and straw) and lowered their buddy down, right in front of Jesus.

Was that an act of faith?

Action

Read Mark 2:1-11 to see what happened next. How did the four friends demonstrate their faith? What compelled them to act this way? What were the results of their faith? Write down your thoughts about how these four friends acted in faith.

Allow the students a few minutes to discuss these questions. As they share, ask the Holy Spirit to give you insight into the fears your students might have.

break it down

Invite students to begin their time alone by praying for the faith of others in the group. Encourage students to go back to their sacred space. Also, some of the students may not be familiar with Brother Andrew, so it may be good to talk briefly about his life as a way to prepare them for their time alone (see www.opendoors.com for more information on Brother Andrew and his ministry).

Do you now have a better understanding of what it means to walk by faith? Read about Brother Andrew, a servant who knows what it means to walk by faith.

GOD'S SMUGGLER

By many people's standards Brother Andrew is crazy. Most of his life, he has smuggled Bibles to people who don't have access to them. On countless occasions he has risked his life because he is faithful to the mission to which God called him. Check out what he said about having faith:

> A huge part of my ministry is to the Christians who are not persecuted, merely intimidated, challenging them to reach out to those who are really suffering. Hebrews 10:32-33 describes two groups in the Body of Christ: those who are persecuted, and those who share in their sufferings. There is no third choice.[6]

What holds you back from helping those who suffer? What stops you from caring for those who experience persecution every day?

Action

Write a letter to God and tell Him what gets in the way of your standing with those who are treated poorly. Talk to Him about your fears and ask Him for opportunities to demonstrate your faith today.

⌇ comeback

Have the students form small groups. After students have shared their Break It Down experience in small groups, ask them to respond to the questions in this section.

Now form small groups and read your letters aloud to each other. If you're alone, find a friend to read your letter to. Then answer these questions together:

- In which areas do you find it hard to follow God and trust Him completely?
- Have you ever experienced persecution? What happened?
- What can you do when you stand in the midst of some kind of persecution?

- Why is it difficult to stand up for your faith when people hurl insults at you or threaten to hurt you?

⌇ project revolution

As students decide on a project, encourage them to choose one that will stretch their faith—a project that will cause them to trust God. Again, you do not want to pressure students into doing something they don't want to do, but encourage them to go outside their own comfort zones in a big way.

Write down several ideas for local research or service projects that you can complete on your own or with your group. The ideas in this section will help get you started.

LEARNING BY EXAMPLE

Think of a person you know whose life of faith you could emulate. Call the person and set up an interview sometime this week to find out more about him or her. Write down 10 questions you would like to ask that person. You may want to invite the person out for lunch or soda. When you get together, pray *with* and *for* the person. Share your interview results at your next group meeting.

SIDEWALK SALE FOR THE POOR

Remember Jesus' words: "If you want to be perfect, go, sell your possessions and give to the poor, and you will have treasure in heaven. Then come, follow me" (Matthew 19:21). With your group, organize a garage, yard or sidewalk sale. Give all the proceeds to a local shelter, homeless ministry or soup kitchen, or give the money away anonymously to someone who needs it.

You don't have a place to hold a garage sale? Instead, go through your belongings and set aside things you no longer need. Think about who could use these things—could you donate your old books to a school or your clothing to a shelter? Could you gather up your unneeded possessions and take them to a thrift store that will sell them and use the money for the poor? Once you've prayed about your project, put it into action!

⩘ momentum

As the session comes to a close, remind the group of the different ways they can go deeper into this topic including the Momentum section on the Soul Survivor Encounter website at www.SoulSurvivor Encounter.com.

Check out these possibilities for going deeper in the Bible this week.

TIME IN THE WORD

Ask the Holy Spirit to give you a deeper faith. May God bless you with inner confidence to outwardly demonstrate your faith to everyone you meet.

Day 1—Proverbs 3:5-6
Day 2—James 1:2-8
Day 3—Joshua 24:14-15
Day 4—Hebrews 13:5-6
Day 5—John 14:1-3

coming to a close

1. Today, ask students to share with their small groups one way they hope to grow in their faith. Ask them to tell the group one thing that God seems to be saying to them as a result of this session.
2. Another option would be to simply have your students choose a prayer partner to pray with as the session ends.
3. Again, you may want to soften the lights and light a candle as a way to focus the prayer at the end.

AFTER THE MEETING

1. **Evaluate**
2. **Encourage**
3. **Equip**
4. **Pray**
5. **Project Revolution**

Note: All leader's options and tips are in shaded areas.

before everyone shows up

1. Pray for each student individually. Ask God to give each student a heart for the world and a desire to share God's love every day.
2. Complete your Project Revolution commitment from the past week.
3. Keep your eyes and ears open during the week for celebrity quotations or interesting stories that demonstrate examples of evangelism or sharing faith. You can use these during the Status section.
4. Gather materials for the study and make sure that all the technology that you will be using, such as a VCR or DVD player, works. Arrange seating so that everyone can see the screen or monitor.
5. Work through the entire session on your own. Highlight the areas that you would like to spend more time with during the study.
6. View the corresponding Soul Survivor video segment ahead of time.
7. Play music and set out food to create a welcoming atmosphere.

GETTING STARTED

1. When people arrive, greet as many as possible and do a quick check-in on their week.
2. Instruct students to share about their project from the previous week.
3. As a group, pray for God's guidance and grace as you complete the study.

Icebreakers

Option 1: As in previous weeks, write out the Scripture passages ahead of time.

Option 2: After everyone arrives, ask students to share their answers to the following questions:
   a. What is the nicest thing someone did for you this week?
   b. What is the nicest thing someone does for you on a regular basis?

Option: For a change this week, have students read through this section on their own and choose one item that they would like to either highlight or ask a question about. It might be a helpful change of pace to let the group's comments and questions guide the discussion for this section.

As you lead the discussion, have students think through the difference between being offended at the message of the gospel and being offended at how the message is given.

WHAT PEOPLE ARE SAYING

SCOTT STAPP, LEAD SINGER, CREED

"We cannot say this enough. We are not a 'Christian band.' We have no agenda to lead others to believe in our specific beliefs . . . Christians around the world distort the true meaning of what Christ said in the Bible—'Let's just love everybody' "[1]

MADONNA, SINGER

"We as Americans are completely obsessed and wrapped up in a lot of the wrong values—looking good, having cash in the bank, being perceived as rich, famous and successful, or just being famous. It's the most superficial part of the American dream and who would know better than me?"[2]

BECK, MUSICIAN

Musician and singer Beck told *Spin* magazine, "My dad's [been] a Scientologist for thirty-five years, my grandfather was a Presbyterian minister, and my mother was raised Jewish, so I've had lots of influences. But whatever."[3]

MEL GIBSON, ACTOR

Mel Gibson talked to an audience about his film *The Passion of the Christ*, "I really feel my career was leading me to make this. The Holy Ghost was working through me on this film, and I was just directing traffic. I hope the film has the power to evangelize."[4]

TOM YORKE, LEAD SINGER, RADIOHEAD

"Having a son has made me very concerned about the future and about how things in the world are being steered. I wonder if our children will even have a future."[5]

DAVE HAVOK, LEAD SINGER, AFI

"Usually, old ladies tell me to find Jesus. Look, I'm just trying to find some chai [tea] and a good vegan muffin."[6]

INTERVIEW

Subject: Liz, former student

For years, if you walked around Buena High School [Ventura, California], you would encounter the "Jesus Lady." From a street corner she told high school students they were destined for hell. In this interview excerpt, you will hear from Liz, a former student who encountered the Jesus Lady.

Soul Survivor: What was your first encounter with the Jesus Lady?

Liz: I got dropped off across the street from school and I heard her yelling, "You are going to hell." Not directly at me personally but at the big group of us walking across the street.

SS: How did she make you feel about God?

L: I was kind of scared. It felt like she was screaming in my face, and I just wanted to say, "Stop screaming at me." It was not a very warm feeling about God. I remember thinking, *If that is who I had to be to follow Christ, then I don't want to follow Christ.*

See the rest of this interview and more thought-provoking quotes at www.SoulSurvivorEncounter.com.

Action

Would you take a course in sharing your faith from the Jesus Lady? If you encountered someone like the Jesus Lady, what would be your natural reaction?

Ask students to share anything they heard this week about how people share their faith with others. Remind them to keep their eyes and ears open for examples of next week's topic, which is perseverance, or how to stay grounded in your faith for the long term.

Discuss: How is the gospel offensive? How do people make the gospel message offensive? What is the difference?

the story

Read this section together and encourage students to ask questions or make comments as you move through the study.

Have you ever known someone who can't stop talking about his or her new boyfriend or girlfriend? Have you ever seen a great movie and told someone else about it? Most people talk about what they love.

People who experience God's love have to tell others about it. Unfortunately, some Christians decide not to talk about Jesus when they see people like the Jesus Lady or a screaming televangelist. Is it possible to share your faith with others without condemning them in the process?

JESUS' LAST WORDS

On an episode of *The Simpsons*, Homer Simpson ate part of a poisonous blowfish, and he thought he was going to die. Homer spent the entire show telling others what was important to him. While most of us have priorities that are different from Homer's, a near-death experience has a way of crystallizing our priorities.

As Jesus prepared to leave His disciples, He gave them some important last words. Check out what Jesus said to Peter the last time they hung out.

> When they had finished eating, Jesus said to Simon Peter, "Simon son of John, do you truly love me more than these?" "Yes Lord," he said, "you know that I love you." Jesus said, "Feed my lambs" (John 21:15).

Jesus wanted Peter to know two things: First, he had been forgiven for denying his Savior three times, and second, he now had a job to do. Jesus asked Peter to take care of people by sharing God's love. Did Jesus ask Peter to yell at people on the street corner? Nope. Did He tell Peter to learn how to argue effectively?

Nope. He asked Peter to care for His sheep.

Establishing a caring relationship with others is the first step in sharing our faith with them. Sharing our faith involves loving people. Just as Jesus came to be our Good Shepherd (see John 10:11), He also sends us out as shepherds to the world (see John 17:18).

The idea of being a shepherd or evangelist is not common in most churches. Most people think that a shepherd is a pastor and an evangelist is one who simply talks about the gospel. Take time to dwell on how caring for someone's soul would naturally lead to speaking about the love of God through Jesus Christ.

Action

Imagine if someone wanted to share God's love with you. How would you like them to do that? In the space provided, describe how you would like someone to share God's love with you.

JESUS' HEART FOR THE WORLD

Four different people told Jesus' story in the Bible: Matthew, Mark, Luke and John. These four writers told the same story, but each one added his personal touch.

In the final chapter of his Gospel, John described how Jesus gave a charge to Peter. In the final chapter of Matthew, Jesus charged all of His disciples. Traditionally, the Church has referred to this passage as the Great Commission because in this passage Jesus passed on a tremendous task to His disciples and to us.

Let's whittle down this passage into bite-sized chunks, so we can grasp the most profound last words ever spoken.

Once again, work through this section with the whole group. Pray that the Holy Spirit would teach and encourage the students as you work through the following bite-sized chunks.

Bite-Sized Chunk 1

> All authority in heaven and on earth has been given to me (Matthew 28:18).

Jesus dispelled any fear the disciples might have had and claimed His ultimate authority. A few days earlier, the disciples had experienced chaos and fear after Jesus' death, and then He told them that He was in total control. Not even death can keep Him down.

Bite-Sized Chunk 2

> Therefore, go and make disciples of all the nations, baptizing them in the name of the Father and of the Son and of the Holy Spirit, and teaching them to obey everything I have commanded you (Matthew 28:19-20).

Jesus pronounced that He was in total control, and yet He still focused on others. Jesus loves all the nations. He sent His disciples—and that includes us—to tell all the nations about His love.

Bite-Sized Chunk 3

> And surely I am with you always, to the very end of the age (Matthew 28:20).

This task requires a supersized God. We can't do it on our own, but Jesus promised to be with us. In fact, He sent the Holy Spirit into the world to help us (see Acts 1:8).

Be sure to dwell a little on this section. Often, when talking about their faith, people either feel very successful or they feel like failures. The truth is that only God can bring someone to Himself. We simply need to be faithful to love others and to speak the truth.

As you prepare this section, think about different experiences you've had where the Holy Spirit has helped you share your faith through actions and words. Be prepared to give some examples if the group needs more direction.

break it down

This week take some time to pray with students before they go off to the Break It Down time. Pray that students would hear from God as they spend time alone with Him. Depending on time, you might gather the group in a circle and have each person pray for the person on his or her left. Another way to pray is for you and/or adult leaders to pray for each student by name before the students go off to find their sacred space.

Take a moment to pray for the others in your group who are about to spend some time with God. Ask the Holy Spirit to bless your time with Him.

JOIN THE HARVEST!

Jesus said, "The harvest is plentiful but the workers are few" (Matthew 9:37). In other words, there is a world full of hurting people but not many people who are willing to share God's love with them. Is God calling you to care for, chat with or show love to certain people? Ask the Holy Spirit to give you insight as you work through the action step.

Action

Write down the names of a couple of people whom God may be calling you to serve, love and pray for. **Note:** Don't stress out if no one comes to mind immediately. Wait for a few minutes. Ask God to open your heart. Write down the names of a few people God may want you to talk with.

comeback

Now get into small groups to discuss your thoughts so far. If you are alone, find a friend and share what you've been thinking about. Discuss the following questions together:

- What fears do you have about serving or talking with others?
- What passage of Scripture in this study speaks to those fears?
- Take time to pray for each other and to ask the Holy Spirit to empower each of you to be an effective witness (in actions and words when necessary) this week.

After discussing the Break It Down section and the Comeback questions, gather the whole group to talk about the common fears involved in sharing our faith. As students share their various fears, write the fears on a large piece of paper or a white board. When the group has spoken all their fears, read Matthew 28:18-20 and ask, "How do Jesus' words impact our specific fears?"

Send the group off to brainstorm ideas for their Project Revolution activity.

≋ project revolution

Write down several ideas for local service projects that you can complete on your own or with your group. The suggestions in this section will help you get started.

CHRISTIANS CAN BE SO OBNOXIOUS

Conduct an informal survey at your school to find out why Christians don't like to talk about their faith or why non-Christians don't like Christians to talk about their faith. Make up a questionnaire with 5 to 10 questions about evangelism, and ask 10 to 12 people to complete it. Share your results at your next group meeting.

BUCKET BRIGADE

Walk around the different stores in your downtown area and offer to wash windows, clean bathrooms or do whatever the store owner or manager needs done. Be sure to ask permission and tell them you are not charging money. Tell them you simply want to serve and help out in the community. Be sure to bring all your own cleaning supplies, and make sure you do a good job. **Note:** This activity is best completed as a group.

≋ momentum

Do you feel that God is calling you to go deeper in your understanding of how to share your faith? Explore the Time in the Word verses on your own.

TIME IN THE WORD

Take time to read each day's passage three times. Each day you can either memorize the verse or write down the passage and carry it around with you, reading it throughout the day. Copy it down in your journal or diary, and then write down what the passage makes you think about.

> **Day 1**—John 17:15-21
> **Day 2**—1 Corinthians 3:5-9
> **Day 3**—2 Corinthians 5:11
> **Day 4**—1 John 1:1-4
> **Day 5**—Psalm 23

coming to a close

1. Have the entire group come back together for prayer. Allow quiet time for students to pray for the people God has been placing on their hearts during the study. Or they could pray with partners or with the whole group.
2. Remind the group that you would love to talk more with them about how to share their faith with others. Also, remind them that you will be praying for them during the week.

AFTER THE MEETING

1. **Evaluate**
2. **Encourage**
3. **Equip**
4. **Pray**
5. **Project Revolution**

Note: All leader's options and tips are in shaded areas.

before everyone shows up

1. Pray for each student individually and for the friends they may invite. Ask God to use this study to encourage them to continue to grow in their faith.
2. Complete your Project Revolution commitment from the past week.
3. Keep your eyes and ears open during the week for celebrity quotations or interesting stories that demonstrate perseverance. You can use these during the Status section.
4. Gather materials for the study and make sure that all the technology that you will be using, such as a VCR or DVD player, works. Arrange seating so that everyone can see the screen or monitor.
5. View the corresponding Soul Survivor video segment ahead of time.
6. Play music and set out food to create a welcoming atmosphere.
7. If you are going to end this study with worship and Communion, make sure to prepare for this ahead of time. Depending on your church's tradition, you many want to invite a pastor to come and serve Communion to your group.

GETTING STARTED

1. When students arrive, check in with the students to see how their week went.
2. Have students share what happened this week as they completed their Project Revolution activities.
3. Pray for God's guidance and grace as you begin this study.

Ask the group if they noticed any quotations or news stories this week that had to do with perseverance, or staying true to your faith over a long period. Remind them that one of the reasons we study the media is that we need to be aware of the messages that are being sent by our culture. One of the hopes for this Status section is to help the students notice what people say and do when it comes to perseverance in their faith.

WHAT PEOPLE ARE SAYING

JASON WADE, LEAD SINGER, LIFEHOUSE

"Religion is the biggest thing that keeps me grounded. It's the backbone to my music and a huge inspiration for my lyrics. It doesn't let all this go to my head, and it helps me realize there's a reason for it all."[1]

ALICIA KEYS, MUSICIAN

"Everything is just thrown on your lap from the time that you're three. The Internet and the TV and the videos and the movies and everything is just like a big soft-porn industry, the entire world. If your elders are acting like that's what they want to do, how are you supposed to think anything else?"[2]

SHAKIRA, SINGER

"The seeds of their education are well-planted in my system. I believe in God. I believe in the sacraments."[3]

FRIEDRICH NIETZCHE, PHILOSOPHER

"What is essential 'in heaven and on earth' seems to be that there should be obedience over a long period of time and in a single direction: given that, something always develops for whose sake it is worthwhile to live."[4]

DAVE GROHL, LEAD SINGER, FOO FIGHTERS

"I'm ever the optimist. I like to think that there's good in everything and that there's light at the end of every tunnel."[5]

INTERVIEW

Subject: Mike Pilavachi, pastor, author and founder of Soul Survivor

Soul Survivor: In your book *Soul Survivor*, you wrote that the Church needs more "deep people." What did you mean by this?

Mike Pilavachi: Sometimes our Christianity can become very religious and superficial. God uses hardships, pain, to bring us closer to Him and to deepen our faith. James 1:3 says, "Consider it pure joy when you face trials of many kinds for the testing of your faith develops perseverance." That verse says it all. I heard someone preach a long time ago that for many people today to live in the victory is simply to be a survivor—that's why we chose the name Soul Survivor for our ministry. We're still surviving. To be honest sometimes it is just hanging in there and knowing there are others praying for you and who understand you.

See the rest of this interview and more thought-provoking quotes at www.SoulSurvivorEncounter.com.

video segment

Show the corresponding Soul Survivor video clip from *Real Life & Undignified Worship DVD*. Before students watch the video, hand out pieces of paper and pens or pencils. Ask them to write down what they feel as they hear what different folks believe about worshiping God.

Option: Show a clip from the movie *Radio* (Columbia Pictures, 2003). This movie tells the story of the relationship between a South Carolina football coach (played by Ed Harris) and a boy described as "the same as everybody else, just a little slower" named Radio (played by Cuba Gooding, Jr.). Show one of the final scenes in which Radio and the coach are talking—after having been friends for 30 years. Their relationship demonstrates the importance of perseverance to gain something wonderful.

As you begin the study, pray for God's guidance and insight into how the group is responding to the material. You may want to read this section with the whole group, have students read the introduction to themselves or have students take turns reading each section aloud.

Would you rather run a 50-yard dash or a marathon? Most people would prefer not to run at all, but that's not an option, so 50 yards or 26 miles?

Before you grab your running shoes and hit the pavement, answer this question: Would it be easier to finish the 50-yard dash or 26 miles? The 50-yard dash is easier because most of us can at least *walk* 50 yards, right?

Now, which would be more satisfying to finish? Without a doubt, even walking a 26-mile marathon would be a worthy accomplishment.

Here's the truth: Walking with Jesus is more like a marathon than a 50-yard dash. God wants to be with you for a lifetime, not just a day, a month or a year. God wants to go the distance with you. Do you want to go the distance with God?

A MAN WITH KNEES LIKE A CAMEL

If someone talked about you after you died, what would you want that person to say? That you looked good, had a great personality and loved people outrageously? How about, "He had knees like a camel"?

Eusebius, who wrote stories about the Early Church, described James, the brother of Jesus, this way: "His knees were calloused like those of a camel from praying for the sins of the people."[6] James stood out from others in that early Christian community—and not just because of his knees! James went the distance with God. Everything he did evidenced passion for Jesus, even his death. When men readied to throw him off the roof of the Temple for speaking about Jesus, which was breaking the law, he continued to pray for people. Since he didn't die from the fall and continued to pray, the men had to crush him with stones.

James knew how to follow Christ for a lifetime, and he wrote a letter to help others follow Christ in the same way. Consider one of the first things he wrote in his letter:

Consider it pure joy, my brothers, whenever you face trials of many kinds, because you know that the testing of your faith develops perseverance. Perseverance must finish its work so that you may be mature and complete, not lacking anything (James 1:2-4).

Before reading the following commentary, ask your students to give their first impressions of this verse. What does this verse make them think about?

James said a few things about the Christian life.

First, he said that it's going to be tough. We will face trials and temptations, and we will live with the fact that life deals some pretty harsh blows.

Second, James said we should think about hard times as a good thing. Why? Because when something tragic happens, we can use that time to strengthen our faith and learn to persevere. Every time we overcome temptation, every time we see God when hard things happen, our lives in Christ deepen. We will mature. We will become more like Jesus.

In fact, if we run this marathon for years, we will experience a depth of joy and satisfaction to which nothing else in life can compare—just as athletes who have worked hard to train for an event and competed successfully.

As you prepare students to think through their temptations and hard life experiences, share a time from your life when you saw God's faithfulness at work.

Action

Now slow down, reflect and write on your faith. What are the main temptations in your life that you find difficult to overcome? How can you work through these temptations with God's help? When you reach 75 years of age and a group of teenagers look at your life, what do you want them to see?

HOW DO YOU GO THE DISTANCE?

Do you remember your first day of middle school?

After you arrived at school, you received a schedule of classes and spent the rest of the day trying to figure out how to get to your next class. Elementary school seemed so much easier. You had one classroom and one teacher who told you everything you needed to know.

At times Bible study can feel the same way. We often hear great words about finding joy in hard times and going the distance, but nobody ever tells us how to actually do it. Fortunately, God's Word tells us exactly what we need to do in order to experience Christ's love in our lives.

In Acts 2:42-47 God gives us a glimpse of how the Holy Spirit guided the Early Church to live. Before reading the passage, we need to realize that when Peter preached his first sermon, about 3,000 people came to know Christ. Now, why didn't they celebrate and move on to the next city? God wanted more than just conversions. He wanted mature disciples. The Early Church developed an attitude of stamina toward walking with Christ.

Action

Read Acts 2:42-47 now. Write down all the ways that members of the Early Church strengthened their relationship with Christ. Are these things easy to do?

Just as it was important to the first Christians, it is also important that we continue to grow in our spiritual maturity and gain wisdom.

Have students share their action answers. The most obvious answers are as follows:

- Reading our Bibles
- Praying with intensity for the Holy Spirit to empower us and others
- Serving other people
- Giving generously
- Seeking God with all our hearts

As you end this section, talk about the spiritual disciplines that you have found most helpful in your own life. Talk honestly about how God has used those disciplines to grow you; also discuss the frustrating aspects involved in staying focused. This will help students complete their Break It Down section.

≣ break it down

Help students realize that they have been practicing a spiritual discipline each week as they have found sacred space. Suggest that they continue to find that space at home. Ask them to think about other areas in their lives where they may need to create a sacred space.

Complete this section individually.

HISTORY MAKERS

James lived more than 2,000 years ago in a small country in the Middle East, and he was killed as a criminal, even though he had lived a just life. Do you find it amazing that James helps you think about going the distance in your faith in Jesus Christ? James, the brother of Jesus, was a history maker, and his letter in the Bible continues to impact countless numbers of people.

The worship song "History Maker" by Martin Smith of the band Delirious? tells how God will use us to make history if we live for Jesus. Jesus will change lives. The song refers to people praying, kings and queens shaking, blind being given sight, miracles happening and people's hearts breaking for God.

This song reminds us that our walk with Christ is about having an impact on other people's lives. History makers don't burn out; rather, they find their strength, hope and energy in running to Jesus daily.

Action

Imagine that a friend were to ask you, "How can I remain faithful to Jesus all my life?" In the space provided, write a letter to your friend and explain how to stay close to Jesus daily. Describe the things you hope to do in the future as a follower of Christ.

≣ comeback

Now get into small groups to read your letters, and then discuss the following questions. If you're alone, read your letter and discuss the questions with a friend or relative.

- How can you stop planning to serve Christ and just go out and do it?
- How do Mike Pilavachi's interview comments apply to your life as a follower of Christ?

≣ project revolution

Encourage small groups to decide on a project that might take a few days to complete.

Write down your ideas for service or research projects that you can do on your own or with your group. The project ideas in this section will help you get started.

MAKE HISTORY ONE LIFE AT A TIME

Think about the different groups on your school campus. Most schools have different groups, or types, of people. Choose a group of people at your school and commit to praying for them with the hope of getting to know them better. Ask God to open up ways for you to make history in their lives. Pray for each person in that group and commit to praying for them for the length of time you're in school. Be prepared to go the distance because God does amazing things!

PRAYER PALS

Many people have pen pals from other countries. Find a prayer pal from another church. Ask God to open the door with someone from another church so that you can pray for each other every day. You may want to exchange e-mail addresses and send out daily prayer requests. You will experience the power of seeing Jesus daily by praying for others, even someone you don't see every day.

≣ momentum

As you come to the end of the Real Life portion of the study, give students a chance to share what extra Momentum features from the website they have found helpful, if any.

If they have not used the information here or the extras on the website, encourage them to go back over the past weeks and look at the options available.

If you want to go even further, use this section to get into the Word this week.

TIME IN THE WORD

Ask God to open your eyes and heart to receive His Word. Each day read the Scripture passage and write down the word, idea or theme that jumps out at you.

Day 1—Psalm 22
Day 2—Ephesians 6:10-18
Day 3—Job 1-2:10
Day 4—Romans 5:1-6
Day 5—Genesis 22:1-14

coming to a close

1. Have each student share something he or she has learned so far and, also, what he or she hopes to continue learning. After everyone shares, take time to pray for each student individually.
2. Encourage the group to join you next week for the next study, which deals solely with worship.

AFTER THE MEETING

1. **Evaluate:** Write down student comments about what they liked and did not like about Real Life so that you can make appropriate adjustments for Undignified Worship.
2. **Encourage:** Try to contact each student during the week, reminding them to join you for part two, Undignified Worship.
3. **Equip:** Complete the next session on your own.
4. **Pray:** Pray for the next session.
5. **Project Revolution:** Complete your own project.

undignified worship

Let Everything That Has Breath

Note: All leader's options and tips are in shaded areas.

before everyone shows up

1. Pray for all the students who will attend and for friends who have been invited.
2. Gather materials for making name tags. Gather magazines, some large index cards and masking or transparent tape.
3. Work through the entire session on your own and mark the areas you would like to focus on during the study. As you prepare, ask God to give you creativity and a heart to listen.
4. Keep your eyes and ears open during the week for relevant celebrity quotations or news stories that demonstrate worship in spirit and truth. You can use these as you go over the Status section with your students.
5. Gather materials for the study and make sure that all the technology that you will be using, such as a VCR or DVD player, works. Arrange seating so that everyone can see the screen or monitor.
6. View the corresponding Soul Survivor video segment ahead of time.
7. Play music and set out food to create a welcoming atmosphere.

GETTING STARTED

1. When students arrive, greet as many as possible and see how their week went.
2. Instruct students to share about their Project Revolution activity from the previous week.
3. Pray for God's guidance and grace as you begin the study.

Icebreakers

Option 1: You may want to prepare slips of papers with Bible references to be read during the meeting. When the students arrive, hand out the passages to be read. Be sensitive to those who may not like to read out loud.

Option 2: Make a commercial. Divide students into three or four smaller groups of no more than eight people. Instruct each group to make up an advertisement for "What People Think Is Important in Life." Give each group a topic beforehand on a slip of paper. Sample topics: fame, money, manipulating crowds, not being bored, doing whatever they please.

Give them five to six minutes to brainstorm and then have each group present their skit to the whole group. The idea here is to get students thinking about why people—and ultimately why they as individuals—do what they do.

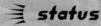
Read through the quotations and the interview excerpt. Have group members alternate reading the quotations and then discuss their reactions.

WHAT PEOPLE ARE SAYING

KELLY OSBORNE, SINGER

"It might sound selfish, but I do whatever makes me happy, as long as I don't hurt anyone."[1]

NICOLE KIDMAN, ACTOR

"When you suddenly become very well-known, there's a deep loneliness to it."[2]

MIKE SHINODA, MUSICIAN, LINKIN PARK

"Even when I was in high school, parties were like, everything is just so played out. You go, people are drinking, you talk to the same people who say the same [stuff]. It's boring. And rather than do that, I could go hang out with my friends and write a new song. And who knows what that's going to be like?"[3]

SONNY SANDOVAL, LEAD SINGER, P.O.D.

"We've never denied our faith or anything—that's something that's with us, with or without rock and roll. All of a sudden people were making an issue out of it. If you are genuine and you want to sit down and talk heart-to-heart, and you care, then we could talk about it. I truly love that."[4]

INTERVIEW

Subject: Andy Hunter, worship leader, DJ
Soul Survivor: Andy, what is worship to you? How is worship in a club or rave venue different from worship at a church or Christian conference?
Andy Hunter: [Worship is] a natural love relationship with Jesus, expressing that passion through my life in God. Sometimes [worship] is a lot harder within church because you are breaking down the norm, having to educate people about [electronic] music and worship; that it doesn't have to be just about singing songs. In the clubs people understand the music, that's why they are there, so I can enjoy myself, mixing and worshiping God, without having

to build a bridge to my audience. Although I have experienced amazing times with God in the church when everyone is going for it and focusing on God, I think that's because we are all outside our comfort zones and that is where God likes to meet us!

See the rest of this interview and more thought-provoking quotes at www.SoulSurvivorEncounter.com.

Ask students if they've heard any news stories or quotations during the week having to do with worship. Also encourage them to keep their eyes and ears open next week for quotations or news stories about why God is worthy of our worship.

 video segment

Show the corresponding Soul Survivor video clip from *Real Life & Undignified Worship DVD*. Before students watch the video, hand out pieces of paper and pens or pencils. Ask them to write down what they feel as they hear what different folks believe about worshiping God.

the story

At this point you can start to prepare students to answer this question: What were you created to do? You may read the Story section yourself, have students alternate reading it or summarize the concepts in your own words. The aim is to get students thinking about motivation at a personal level.

WHY ARE WE HERE?

The word "why" is a powerful word. When you ask yourself why you do the things you do, you ask a fundamental question of life: What is your purpose in life? As you know, answering this question isn't easy. What motivates people to do what they do?

Now personalize this question. What motivates you every day? Ask yourself why you do the simplest actions. Maybe your day goes something like this:

> Got up this morning and put on jeans and a
> T-shirt. Why?
> So people wouldn't laugh at me. Why?
> So I get a good education and attend a good
> college. Why?
> So I can get a good job. Why?
> So I can enjoy my life, earn money and have
> stuff. Why?

Action

In the space provided, write down a few of your daily actions. After you write down each action, answer the question Why? (Follow the example above.) Have you come to any conclusions? Why do you do what you do? Sum it up in one sentence.

WHY DO WE WORSHIP?

The Bible says a lot about motivation, honesty and why we do the things we do. As you read 1 Peter 2:9, circle a word or phrase from the verse that describes what you were created to do.

> But you are a chosen people, a royal priesthood, a holy nation, a people belonging to God, that you may declare the praises of him who called you out of darkness into his wonderful light (1 Peter 2:9).

Maybe you picked "chosen people," "royal priesthood," "holy nation," or "a people belonging to God." Good. But what if you picked the word "that," as in: "a people belonging to God that you may declare the praises of him." Why might the word "that" be so important? In a way, the whole verse hinges on this word. We're a people belonging to God that we might declare His praises. In other words, the reason God created us is to worship Him.

Why did God create us to worship Him? The biblical foundation of worship is God's immense worth. Check out Psalm 150:2, which says, "Praise God in his sanctuary; . . . praise him for his surpassing greatness," and Psalm 150:6, which says, "Let everything that has breath praise the LORD." God is so amazing, so incredible and so wonderful that all of creation—us included—is meant to bring glory to Him. Our lives are meant to be worship to God.

Action

How do others worship God with their whole lives? Write a short phrase about how each of the following individuals worshiped God:

> Dorcas (see Acts 9:36)
> Sons of Asaph (see 1 Chronicles 25:1)
> Miriam (see Exodus 15:20)
> Jesus (see Matthew 14:23)

WHAT DOES THAT MEAN?

According to 1 Peter 2:9, our purpose on Earth is to bring glory to God, but what does that really mean to you? How does that affect your everyday life?

Action

Let's start by taking the following quiz. For each statement below, check True or False. Be prepared to give your reasons. Check your answers at the end of the session.

1. Worship only happens when we sing.
   ❑ True   ❑ False
2. You can worship anybody that's beautiful and true.
   ❑ True   ❑ False
3. You must be in church to worship God.
   ❑ True   ❑ False
4. You can worship God at school.
   ❑ True   ❑ False
5. You must be in a group to worship.
   ❑ True   ❑ False
6. You can worship the Lord by being silent.
   ❑ True   ❑ False

Let's discover the true definition of worship. Jesus said in Luke 4:8, "It is written: 'Worship the Lord your God and serve him only.'" This simple statement lays some groundwork for our definition of worship. We may admire people when they're beautiful and true; but based on this verse, the only being we are to worship is God.

≋ break it down

If you have room, encourage students to find their sacred space. At this point discuss the transition into the practical aspects of worshiping God on a daily basis.

Complete this section individually.

DEFINING WORSHIP

In Psalm 96, worship is given quite a rousing description. This passage outlines a number of actions that express our praise to God, such as singing, declaring His glory, coming into His courts, proclaiming His name and rejoicing.

In this activity, students will develop their own definitions for worship. Allowing them to do this in their own words may feel strange, particularly if the group features a variety of kids. You may have to guide students back to the descriptions of worship found in Psalm 96. The point here is to encourage them to describe worship in their own words—ways that they can understand and live out.

Action

Read all of Psalm 96. In your own words, write a short definition of worship based on the description given in these verses.

WORSHIP ANYWHERE

Check out Colossians 3:17: "Whatever you do, whether in word or deed, do it all in the name of the Lord Jesus." Does this verse say that worship is a song we can only sing in church? No. This verse indicates that wherever we are, whatever we do can be done for the glory of God.

Action

List five things you can do every day to worship God at home, work or school. How can you worship Him without using your voice? How can you worship God at school or with your friends?

Worshiping God as a holistic lifestyle may be a new concept to some students and may need clarity. Discuss the importance of reverence when developing fresh definitions of daily acts of worship.

⋚ comeback

Have students form small groups of six to eight to discuss their Break It Down answers.

Now get into small groups and discuss your action answers. Also discuss the following questions together. If you're working alone, find a friend, parent or someone else close to you and discuss the things you're thinking about.

- What is worship all about? How can we worship more fully?
- If we don't know how to worship or don't know what to say when we pray or sing,

how does the Holy Spirit help us? Hint: Read Romans 8:26-27.
- How can living to worship God affect the choices you make?
- Spend some time as a group praying for one another. Pray that each of you would know what it means to worship God in everyday life.

⋚ project revolution

Keep students in the small groups and have them come up with a project they will accomplish before the meeting next week. Remind them that this project is to be completed outside the church walls.

Write down your ideas for projects that you can complete outside the church walls. Choose a project to put into action this week.

WORSHIP DAY

Pick one day this week and designate it as Worship Day. Worship God through your actions all day. Can you glorify God while brushing your teeth? How can you glorify God at breakfast time? Maybe you can focus on serving others, not complaining, or praying for God's guidance during the day. At the end of the day, make a short list of your activities and then list how you tried to glorify God through each one. Share your list with your group when you meet again. Remember, this is something you can do every day.

PRAYER LIST

Make a list of friends you can pray for. Pray that they would know what it means to worship God in everyday life. Put the prayer list on your bedroom wall, in your car, in your backpack, or in your wallet or purse. Keep the list handy all week, and renew the list at the end of the week, adding new names to pray for.

⋚ momentum

As the session comes to a close, remind students that there are many ways to go deeper into this topic. As always, refer them to the Soul Survivor Encounter website, www.SoulSurvivorEncounter.com, for more Momentum recommendations.

Also, students are a great resource for locating the most current websites and periodicals.

If you want to go further, read the suggestions in this section to help you get started.

TIME IN THE WORD

Read the following passages this week as part of your time with God. Write out your thoughts about what you've read.

Day 1—Habakkuk 3:17-18
Day 2—Philippians 3:3
Day 3—John 4:23-24
Day 4—Psalm 100:1
Day 5—Psalm 150

coming to a close

1. Have students come back together for prayer. Again, they can either pray in partners or pray together as a group. Have index cards available for students to write down their prayer requests.
2. You may want to soften the lights and light a candle before you move into prayer.

AFTER THE MEETING

1. **Evaluate:** Leaders should spend time evaluating the meeting's effectiveness. Take time to talk about how God worked, what went well and what did not go well. Take notes for next week's meeting.
2. **Encourage:** During the week try to contact your students (phone calls, notes of encouragement, e-mails or instant messages), and let them know you are praying for them. Also find out about their prayer requests. Be very intentional on following up with students who committed or recommitted themselves to following Christ recently.
3. **Equip:** Complete the next session.
4. **Pray:** Prayerfully prepare for the next meeting.
5. **Project Revolution:** Complete your own project.

Quiz Answers
(1) False, (2) False, (3) False, (4) True, (5) False, (6) True

I'll Bring You More Than a Song

Note: All leader's options and tips are in shaded areas.

before everyone shows up

1. Pray for all the students who will attend and for friends who have been invited.
2. Work through the entire session on your own ahead of time and mark the areas that you would like to focus on during the study. As you prepare, ask God to give you creativity and a heart to listen.
3. Keep your eyes and ears open during the week for relevant celebrity quotations or news stories that demonstrate the difference between music and worship. You can use these as you go over the Status section with your students.
4. Gather materials for the study and make sure that all the technology that you will be using, such as a VCR or DVD player, works. Arrange seating so that everyone can see the screen or monitor.
5. View the corresponding Soul Survivor video segment ahead of time.
6. Play music and set out food to create a welcoming atmosphere.

GETTING STARTED

1. When students begin to arrive, greet as many as possible and catch up.
2. Pray for God's guidance and grace in leading students through this session.

Icebreaker

You may want to prepare slips of papers with Bible references to be read during the meeting. When students arrive hand out the passages to be read. Be sensitive to those who may not like to read out loud.

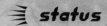

WHAT PEOPLE ARE SAYING

BONO, LEAD SINGER, U2

"I don't think religion has anything to do with God anymore or very rarely has. It is also becoming clear that the material world is not enough for anybody. We had a century of being told by the intelligentsia that we're two-dimensional creatures, that if something can't be proved, it can't exist. That's over now. Transcendence is what everybody, in the end, is on their knees for, running at speed toward, scratching at, kicking at."[1]

ZACHARY LEVI, ACTOR

The costar of ABC's sitcom *Less Than Perfect* talked about landing a spot on the show: "It felt as if God was saying, 'I want to give you this, but I need to know that you are able to handle that blessing. With great blessing comes great responsibility.'"[2]

SEAN "P. DIDDY" COMBS, HIP-HOP ARTIST

"I believe in God. He's my best friend. If I truly have belief and have faith, why would I be afraid to meet God? I mean, what would I fear? If something happens to me, he's just calling me to leave."[3]

BEYONCÉ KNOWLES, SINGER

"I'm definitely spiritual. God plays a huge part in my life. I owe all of my happiness and success to Him."[4]

INTERVIEW

Subject: Matt Redman, worship leader, author
Prolific songwriter Matt Redman wrote the songs "Better Is One Day" and "Heart of Worship" and the books *The Unquenchable Worshipper* and *Facedown*, both available from Regal Books.

Soul Survivor: Is it true you always used to sing at the back of church? Is it easier to worship God from the back?

Matt Redman: I guess it's just that I'm not very naturally an up-front person. I'd rather hide away at the back because of my personality. But the cool thing about worshiping at the back is you get a little glimpse of everyone else too, which can be a massively encouraging thing at times.

See the rest of this interview and more thought-provoking quotes at www.SoulSurvivorEncounter.com.

video segment

Show the corresponding Soul Survivor video clip from *Real Life & Undignified Worship DVD*. Before students watch the video, hand out pieces of paper and pens or pencils. Ask them to write down what they feel as they hear what different folks believe about worshiping God.

Option: Show a clip from Mel Gibson's film *The Passion of the Christ*. Show the scene where Jesus is carrying the cross and falls down hard. His mother Mary is watching, and she thinks back to a time when he fell down as a little boy. Make sure this scene is appropriate for the age of the group you're leading.

the story

Summarize the concepts presented in this section or have group members alternate reading the narrative. You may want to have each student participate in the Six Degrees of Separation game individually (if they didn't complete it prior to the meeting) or do one large-scale game up front with four to six students.

Do you think it would be difficult to call the president of the United States or the prime minister of the United Kingdom? Could you simply snap open your cell phone, hit speed dial and get him on the line? No way. Maybe the governor or another regional leader could make the phone call. But let's face it—calling the leader of a country is not easy.

SIX DEGREES FROM CELEBRITY

Have you heard of the game Six Degrees of Separation? The idea of this game is this: You can connect yourself to anyone on Earth through only six other people. For example: Maybe you know somebody who knows somebody else and suddenly, six people later, you connect with someone who knows the president of the United States.

Try and sketch out a list of people you know who could connect you to the president, prime minister or another celebrity.

Action

Try to connect yourself to a celebrity in fewer than six moves:

I know

_____ (1)

He/she knows

_____ (2)

He/she knows

_____ (3)

He/she knows

_____ (4)

He/she knows

_____ (5)

He/she knows this celebrity

_____ (6)

ENCOUNTERING GOD

Continue to summarize the following concepts or have students read portions of the text.

Even though world leaders are tough men to get in touch with, their own families have constant access to them. The president's family can talk to him at any time because of their relationship with him.

We have the same kind of unlimited access to someone even more amazing, not just the president of a country. He is the King of life, the creator of the universe and Lord of heaven and Earth. He is God.

How do we know we have unlimited access to God? Again, we know because of our relationship with Him. When Jesus Christ went to the cross, He broke down the barrier between humankind and God.

The Bible says that God sent His Son so that we could be called His children (see Galatians 4:4-5; 1 John 3:1). And just like the president's family has access to him through their relationship with him, we have unlimited access to God through the power of the Holy Spirit. Check out this verse: "In him and through faith in him we may approach God with freedom and confidence" (Ephesians 3:12).

Action

Think about that for a moment. You can approach God, the ultimate being, at any time. Write out your thoughts on encountering the God of the universe. What questions would you ask God if you were standing right next to Him? (Ask Him your questions right now!) How does this idea of approaching God apply to worship?

To flesh out the idea of access to God, walk students through Matthew 27:51 and Luke 23:44-45, which recount how the Temple's curtain was torn in two as Christ died. The curtain separated the holy of holies from the rest of the Temple. Why was it torn? Because of Christ's death, people now have direct access to God—we no longer have to go through a sacrificial system. Christ was the only sacrifice needed to enable people to have a proper relationship with God. See also Romans 5:2.

WHAT IS THE HEART OF WORSHIP?

Let's draw a distinction between music and worship. Music is a vehicle by which we can worship God. It is an important vehicle because we all have preferences when it comes to what type of music we enjoy. But music itself is not worship. Music carries the essence of our hearts to God. When our hearts overflow with love for God, we can express that praise in any number of ways—one of those ways is through song. Worship can also be expressed in many other ways.

How can we define real worship? We worship when we encounter God. When we get to know who He is, our hearts respond to His greatness, majesty, justice, truth and perfection. That's real, true, authentic worship. Sometimes we respond to God in song. But worship is more than a song; it's a worshipful attitude of reverence for God that comes directly from our hearts.

Action

Take a few minutes to complete the following sentences in your own words:

- God, when I think about encountering you I feel . . .

- Jesus, when I sing songs of worship to you I'm thinking about . . .
- In my heart, my attitude during worship is . . .

- Psalm 100
- Isaiah 29:13
- John 4:23-24
- Romans 12:1-2
- Ephesians 2:18

It can be a shocking experience when people truly grasp what it means to talk to God. This is particularly true if students have grown up in church and become familiar with prayer and worship. Jesus can become so common to them that they forget who they're actually addressing. To help introduce this idea of talking to God, play a lyrically powerful worship song to enunciate the point.

⋛ break it down

If you run into some extreme reactions to the following quiz, don't panic. It is not uncommon today for Christians of any age to believe that music and worship are the same things. The purpose of this quiz is to help squash that fallacy.

Again, have students find their own space where they can complete this activity.

Take 10 minutes and complete this section's activity individually.

IN SPIRIT AND TRUTH

The Bible says that worshiping God happens in our spirits and cannot be made up of constricting rules and regulations. That means our expression of worship to God—whether we're singing in church, serving the poor, respecting our parents or even washing someone's car—is a reflection of our attitude before God. Psalm 100 binds worship to gladness and joy, both sincere attitudes of the heart. But you wouldn't make a rule for your worship time that says: You can only worship when you feel joyful. Worship springs from our true selves; even if we're lamenting or grieving, we can sincerely worship the Lord.

Action

What does the Bible say about encountering God when you worship? Look up the following verses and write out their meanings in your own words in the space provided:

⋛ comeback

As before, form small groups for the Comeback time. Allow each group to discuss their Break It Down answers and then discuss the following questions. The idea is to give them focus while worshiping God, so they can sincerely set their minds on things above (see Colossians 3:2).

Now get into groups of two or three and share your descriptions of the Scriptures you just read. If you are working alone, find someone to share your thoughts with. Then discuss the following questions:

- What does it mean to have access to God?
- How do you define the difference between worship and music?
- How can you sincerely worship God if you don't like the music?

Worshiping God is a practical and valuable lesson to teach students, regardless of the type of music. The idea, again, is that the music is only a vehicle to worship. True worship is an attitude of the heart. No matter what the music style or method, a person can still encounter God.

⋛ project revolution

The idea for this Project Revolution is for students to be able to worship God even when a worship experience does not correspond directly to their personal preferences. Tell each small group that next week they are going to report on the project they completed. You may also want to do this week's project with the whole group at someone's house. Doing one of these projects together can create a spirit of unity.

Write down your ideas for service or research projects that you can do alone or with your group. Choose an idea that you or your group will put into action this week. Read the suggestions in this section to get you thinking about your project.

GENERATIONAL WORSHIP

With your small group, hold a time of generational worship at somebody's house. Here's how: The challenge is for your group to be able to worship God sincerely, despite some obstacles. Pick up a bunch of old reading glasses at a thrift store and buy a bag of cotton balls. Have everyone in your group put on a pair of the old glasses and stuff cotton balls in everyone's ears. Next, pick out a bunch of songs nobody knows. Have the group sing three or four songs while no one can hear or see very well. When the time of worship is over, talk about what it was like as a group. Share your experience at your next meeting.

INTERACTIVE PRAYER LIST

Make a short list of friends or relatives you can pray for. Put a friend's or relative's name on your list if he or she is dealing with a problem or struggling with a particular issue. Keep this prayer list with you all week: at school, band practice, soccer practice or work—wherever you are during the week. Pray that your friends or relatives would have freedom and confidence to approach God. At the end of the week, call the people on your list and ask them how they are doing. Let them know you've been thinking about them and praying for them, whatever their situation might be. Tell them that you will continue to pray for them. Follow up with your small group next week and let them know how it went!

≋ momentum

Promoting Scripture references for further study can be one way of encouraging daily Scripture reading for students. As the session comes to a close, remind them that if they want to go deeper this week, there are many ways to do that. Let them know what you will be doing during the week to go deeper.

If you want to go further, the verses in this section will get you started.

TIME IN THE WORD

Set aside 10 minutes a day and write your thoughts on the following passages:

Day 1—Isaiah 6:1-5
Day 2—Ezekiel 1
Day 3—Psalm 99
Day 4—Psalm 32
Day 5—Jeremiah 17:14

review

The Unquenchable Worshipper, by Matt Redman

In chapter eight of his new book, Matt Redman writes "in a potentially hypnotizing world, the challenge for undivided worshippers is to keep their eyes fixed on Jesus—simple to define perhaps but in practice not quite so easy." This is one of the many challenges to a person striving to live a life of worship that Redman addresses. In this concise but impassioned book, Redman challenges his readers to come back to "the heart of worship" and become the types of people who desire every aspect of their lives to be acceptable offerings unto God.

Using an abundance of Scripture as well as a vast array of people's stories throughout history, Redman does more than just define what it takes to worship with wonderful passion, he also describes what it takes to worship with an unpredictable, unstoppable, unending vigor; in other words, "unquenchable." The reader encounters the extravagance of Charles Wesley, the relentlessness of Stephen as he faced martyrdom, the private worship of King David, and many other great biblical and historical examples that truly give us a glimpse of what it takes to really worship God in spirit and in truth.

Many times we read definitions of worship that attempt to teach us how to worship; but Matt Redman's book has taken the definitions a step further and shows us through the lives of others that ultimate, lifelong worship combines many attributes that we should all strive for. *The Unquenchable Worshipper* is a short enough book that anyone can find time to read and anyone desiring to enter the heart of worship should definitely read this book.[5]

coming to a close

1. Have the group come back together for prayer. This time, invite students to write down their prayers on a large piece of butcher paper. Allow students to scrawl their prayers anywhere along the paper, and tell them that you will be posting it on the wall so that they can check on it periodically.

2. As before, you may want to soften the lights, light a candle or even put on some music before you move into this prayer journaling time.

AFTER THE MEETING

1. **Evaluate**
2. **Encourage**
3. **Equip**
4. **Pray**
5. **Project Revolution**

Note: All leader's options and tips are in shaded areas.

before everyone shows up

1. Pray for the students who will attend the meeting and for friends they may invite.
2. Complete your own personal Project Revolution commitment from last week.
3. Work through the entire session on your own and mark the areas on which you would like to spend more time.
4. Keep your eyes and ears open during the week for celebrity quotations or interesting stories that demonstrate how people worship. You can use these in the Status section.
5. Gather materials for the study and make sure that all the technology that you will be using, such as a VCR or DVD player, works. Arrange seating so that everyone can see the screen or monitor.
6. View the corresponding Soul Survivor video segment ahead of time.
7. Play music and set out food to create a welcoming atmosphere.

GETTING STARTED

1. **Option:** Play a DVD of a Soul Survivor worship event.
2. When everyone arrives, ask students to introduce themselves to someone they haven't met by telling the person about a worship song they love and a worship song they hate and why. Give them a few minutes to chat.
3. Let each small group share what happened with their Project Revolution activity.
4. Pray for God's guidance and grace as you begin the study.

Icebreaker

Option 1: React. Divide the students into two teams—the Incident group and the Response group—and give each team 15 to 20 slips of paper and a pen. Instruct the Incident group to write one sentence on each slip of paper that shows two people in a cause-and-effect situation, followed by this question: How do you respond?

For example: "Your father just gave you a new car. How do you respond?" Or "Your teacher gave you an F on your final exam. How do you respond?"

Instruct the Response group to write one sentence on each slip of paper that features a reaction, starting with the phrase: "You respond by . . ."

For example: "You respond by arguing and screaming." Or "You respond by running around in a circle and yelling 'Wow!'"

Finally, put all the slips of paper into two piles, mix them up and have brave students pick one slip of paper from each pile, reading the first paper and acting out the response in front of the group.

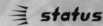 **status**

WHAT PEOPLE ARE SAYING

LAURYN HILL, MUSICIAN

"Talking about God doesn't embarrass me. It doesn't make me less cool or less popular or make me corny."[1]

LENNY KRAVITZ, MUSICIAN

"People want to be loved and want to love. That is what we were put here for. That is what we were created to do."[2]

SEAN "P. DIDDY" COMBS, MUSICIAN

"I was thinking how truly blessed I am. I give all glory to God."[3]

TOM PETTY, MUSICIAN

"I don't believe in censorship, but I do believe that an artist has to take some moral responsibility for what he or she is putting out there. And I think a lot of these young kids are going to have to learn the hard way before they realize that you can actually do some damage if you're being careless or frivolous in what you're saying."[4]

INTERVIEW

Subject: Greg Russinger, worship leader, pastor
Soul Survivor: Have you written any new songs lately?
Greg Russinger: Yes, actually I have. There was an earthquake just recently, and I was eating breakfast with my family in a local restaurant. As the earthquake hit, people got up panicking, others were shouting, while others dove under their tables. As I watched (and rode the earthquake) I thought of the many natural elements that cause unrest and fear. The next day I found myself writing a song entitled "Moved by You."
SS: What does the word "worship" mean to you?

GR: Initiation. God's pursuit of humanity (you and me) found throughout the biblical story refashions the heart. When we surrender to this pursuit daily, all of life becomes a pursuit of God, the worship of His worthiness.

See the rest of this interview and more thought-provoking quotes at www.SoulSurvivorEncounter.com.

 video segment

Show the corresponding Soul Survivor video clip from *Real Life & Undignified Worship DVD.* Before students watch the video, hand out pieces of paper and pens or pencils. Ask them to write down what they feel as they watch the clip.

the story

Have students alternate reading this section aloud, or summarize the concepts yourself.

Recently, a simple prank turned deadly in an Amish community in Ohio. Each year, as a kind of odd tradition, students hide in cornfields and hurl tomatoes at passing cars. This year on Labor Day a motorist who had been pelted by a tomato or two got out of his car and fired 3 to 5 shots into the 7-foot-high corn, killing a 23-year-old young man.

The group with the young man told the sheriff they had been throwing tomatoes at passing vehicles and gave a vague description of a middle-aged male of medium height. Residents reeled in shock, unable to understand why anybody would respond so violently.[5]

Action

Answer the following questions about the story you just read: What response do you think the students expected from the passing motorists? What happened instead? Do you always get the response you hope for? Do you always respond the way others expect you to?

WORSHIP IS A RESPONSE

Merriam-Webster's Collegiate Dictionary defines the word "response" this way: "1: to say something in return 2: something constituting a reply or a reaction."[6] How can we apply the concept of response to worshiping God?

When we encounter God, we discover His character and get to know who He is. Our hearts are forced to respond to His greatness, majesty, justice, truth and perfection.

Action

Take a few minutes to read the following verses and answer the accompanying questions:

- Read Romans 5:6-10. When we worship God, what are we responding to?
- Read Nehemiah 9:5-6. Why do we worship God? (Give at least two reasons.)
- Read Psalm 57:5. Where is God's glory?

RESPONDING TO GOD

What does it mean to respond to God in worship? Usually something triggers your thoughts about God. You respond in your spirit when you think about God because real worship happens in your heart. That attitude of your heart causes you to think, feel, pray, cry, dance, sing, shout, speak, lie down on the ground or fast. These attitudes manifest themselves as signs of worship.

You stand on a mountain peak looking out at miles and miles of the horizon—it's an incredible view. When you think about the view, you also enjoy the creator of the view. You might even praise God for His beauty. That's worship.

Maybe you just read several passages in the Bible about the holiness and perfection of God. These verses cause you to feel remorseful about sinful actions in your life. You confess your sins and praise Him as He reminds you that He is ever loving and always forgiving. That's worship.

Perhaps you gave food to the homeless or volunteered in a homeless shelter with some of your time. Maybe you helped your brother with his homework, gave money to a poor family or tutored a child. Jesus said, "Whoever welcomes a little child in my name welcomes me" (see Matthew 18:5). That's worship!

Depending on the age and spiritual maturity of the group members, you may want to create your own examples of worship similar to those from the previous section. Reiterate here that the heart is the center of a person's will, emotions, motivations and being. As discussed in the previous section, worship is more than just singing a song; worship is a sincere response of one's heart.

≣ break it down

Take some time to complete this section's activity individually.

REPORTING LIVE

In the Old Testament, Isaiah paints a majestic picture of an encounter with God in chapter 6. Can you imagine what it would be like to stand in God's holy presence? Then, out of the corner of your eye, you spot these six-winged, angelic seraphs hovering over a temple, simultaneously covering their faces, their feet, flying and singing? Whoa!

Action

Read Isaiah 6:1-7. Imagine you're a reporter for a major newspaper, standing next to the prophet Isaiah and experiencing this amazing encounter with God. In the space provided, write a news article about what happens to you (the reporter) as you stand with Isaiah.

When? In what year did this happen?
Where? Where was the Lord seated?
Who? Whom did you see with Him?
What? What did it look like? What did the seraphs say?
Why? Why did Isaiah respond the way he did?
How? How did the seraph demonstrate the atonement of Isaiah's guilt?

≣ comeback

Read the following verses and discuss the questions with your group or find a friend, parent or relative with whom you can talk through these questions.

- Read Romans 5:6-10. When we worship God, what are we responding to?
- Read Nehemiah 9:5-6. Why do we worship God? (Give at least two reasons.)

- Read Psalm 57:5. Where is God's glory?
- Read Ephesians 3:1. What is one reason to praise God?

project revolution

Write down ideas for service projects that you can complete outside the church walls. Choose one that you or your group will put into action this week. Read the suggestions in this section to help get you started.

RESPONSE ART

On your own or with your small group, create some "response art." This could be a collage, poster or three-dimensional creation that illustrates your response to God's character. Pick one of God's attributes such as His holiness, love or power, and create your art piece with that theme in mind. The idea is to remind people of the attribute of God that you chose. Be creative. Use words, shapes and phrases, or glue together household items like fabrics or cardboard. Bring your piece to your next group meeting.

REAL SERVICE

Find a senior citizens' center near your home. Call up the director, supervisor or manager and ask him or her if you or your group can do anything to help the residents who live there. Perhaps you can complete a maintenance project. Maybe you can host a service with songs they'll enjoy or with short testimonies of God's greatness. Perhaps you can simply go there and talk with the residents who feel lonely.

momentum

If you want to go further, the Time in the Word verses will get you started.

TIME IN THE WORD

Read the following passages this week as part of your time with God. In your journal, pencil in your thoughts about the verses you've just read.

coming to a close

1. Bring students back together for prayer. Instruct them to spend some quiet time praying for the people God has placed on their hearts during the session. You may want to have them pray with partners or with the whole group.
2. Remind students that you would love to talk more with them about different avenues of worshiping God.

AFTER THE MEETING

1. **Evaluate**
2. **Encourage**
3. **Equip**
4. **Pray**
5. **Project Revolution**

Note: All leader's options and tips are in shaded areas.

before everyone shows up

1. Pray for the students who will attend and for friends they may invite.
2. Complete your own Project Revolution commitment from last week.
3. Work through the entire session on your own and mark the areas that you would like to spend more time on during the study.
4. Keep your eyes and ears open during the week for relevant celebrity quotations or news stories that demonstrate worship or the presence of God.
5. Gather materials for the study and make sure that all the technology that you will be using, such as a VCR or DVD player, works. Arrange seating so that everyone can see the screen or monitor.
6. View the corresponding Soul Survivor video segment ahead of time.
7. Play music and set out food to create a welcoming atmosphere.

GETTING STARTED

1. Let each small group share what they did this past week for their Project Revolution activity and what happened.
2. Pray for God's guidance and grace as you begin the study.

Icebreakers

Option 1: Prepare slips of paper with Bible references that can be read during the meeting. When students arrive, hand out the passages to be read aloud. Be aware of those who may not like to read out loud.

Option 2: Divide the students into partners or groups of three or four. Have them answer the questions: Right now, if you weren't at youth group, if you could be anywhere, doing anything, where would you be? What would you be doing? After the small groups have had two to three minutes to discuss, invite discussion with the whole group.

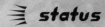

WHAT PEOPLE ARE SAYING

MARY J. BLIGE, SINGER

"When people tell me that I saved their lives, that's a compliment, because what they don't know is that I'm trying to save my own life. I'm crying out for help, and I'm saving somebody else."[1]

JOHNNY CASH, MUSICIAN

Cash talked to an interviewer in 2002 about his brush with death: "My faith held up beautifully. I never questioned God, I never doubted God, I never got angry at God. I can't understand people saying they got angry at God. I walked with God all the way through all this. That's why I didn't fear. I never feared anything. Not at all. I can honestly say that."[2]

ALAN JACKSON, MUSICIAN

When asked about his post-September 11 song "Where Were You (When the World Stopped Turning)," Jackson said, "God wrote it, I just held the pencil." [3]

BOB DYLAN, MUSICIAN

"I've always thought there's a superior power, that this is not the real world and that there's a world to come. That no soul has died, every soul is alive, either in holiness or in flames. And there's probably a lot of middle ground."[4]

INTERVIEW

Subject: Kendall Payne, worship leader, musician
Singer and songwriter Kendall Payne broke onto the music scene with her major label debut *Jordan's Sister*. Her songs have been featured on the TV shows *Felicity*, *Popular*, *Wasteland* and *Providence*.
Soul Survivor: How do you know God is real in your life? How, where or through whom do you experience God?
Kendall Payne: I feel Him and experience Him in every detail of my day. I see Him in the mechanic who fixes my car, in the steam that rises from my cup of coffee, in the seasons changing from sum-

mer to fall, in my friend B's high-pitch laugh, in modern inventions like TV or the refrigerator, in a mother feeding her baby. He is everywhere if I have the eyes to see Him.

See the rest of this interview and more thought-provoking quotes at www.SoulSurvivorEncounter.com.

After the discussion of the Status interview and quotations, highlight which comment or quote you found most interesting and invite discussion from students.

video segment

Show the corresponding Soul Survivor video clip from *Real Life & Undignified Worship DVD*. Before students watch the video, hand out pieces of paper and pens or pencils. Ask them to write down what they feel as they watch the clip.

the story

Have students alternate reading the following section, or summarize it yourself.

NOWHERE ELSE I'D RATHER BE

Have you ever really wanted to be somewhere? Consider this:

> For 11 weeks every summer, 35 or so 16-year-olds scrub pots and pans, mop shower houses, clean toilets, rake beaches and get blisters from clearing hiking trails. These students don't get paid to work at their summer job. They pay to work. Why would anybody do that?
> Camp Firwood, in Washington, has run its Counselor-in-Training (C.I.T.) program for decades on a pay-to-work basis. Teens (or their parents) pay tuition for what is described as one of the best youth-development programs in the United States. Besides the hard work, teens water-ski, ride horses and compete in extreme competitions.

Think for a moment. Where would you really like to be right now?
Maybe you want to visit a geographical place like

Hawaii or the Swiss Alps. Maybe you hope for a new position at school such as head cheerleader or captain of the football team. Maybe you're ready to enter a new stage of life like graduating from high school and going to college or getting your braces off.

IN GOD'S PRESENCE

One of King David's music ministers wrote a song to God about where he wanted to be. He wrote these words: "Better is one day in your courts than a thousand elsewhere" (Psalm 84:10). Out of all the amazing things the songwriter had undoubtedly seen and experienced in the world, he only wanted to be in the presence of God.

Just like this music minister, we enter into the presence of the almighty God, the creator of the universe, the King of kings, the Lord of lords when we worship Him. How incredible is that?

Sometimes we forget how it feels to be in God's presence. We can sing phrases like "God is great" or songs about how we long to be in God's presence, but do we honestly believe it? Some people might choose to sit on a beach in Jamaica or hang out with friends rather than sit in God's presence. Maybe that's because they don't truly know what it means to be with God. Here's the point: While things on Earth are beautiful, striking and spectacular, God is even greater.

Remind yourself of something spectacular in life that you love. When you think of something spectacular, your understanding of God can take on a whole new perspective.

The reality for many believers is that we simply forget that we're worshiping God. God is a God of utmost glory—but how do we truly know, feel and act upon what that means?

Action

Complete the following statements:

- When I'm hungry, I love to eat . . .
- If I could drive any vehicle in the world, I'd drive a . . .
- In my free time, my favorite thing to do is . . .
- If I could travel anywhere, I'd go to . . .
- The most incredible natural creation I've seen is . . .

- I want to fall in love with a person who looks like . . .
    and acts like . . .
    and is totally . . .
- The most spectacular thing I can think of is . . .

The point of the favorite metaphor exercise is to turn the concept of the spectacular into something tangible for students. Once they start thinking of how great their favorite car is, introduce the idea that God is even better than the car. To the seasoned believer this may sound obvious, even irreverent, but we want to help students turn the corner here. We want them to grasp a tiny portion of the incredible glory of God.

AN INCREDIBLE GOD

Now think about all the things you listed above. Combine those things in your head and think about this short sentence: God is better still. When you worship God, remember that He is truly the best thing we can think of or imagine. Compared with anything on Earth that we think of as excellent, God is better still.

For thousands of years people have used comparisons to describe their longing for God. Check out Psalm 42:1: "As the deer pants for streams of water, so my soul pants for you, O God."

Action

Read through your list again. Think about one or two of your favorite things; then write your own sentence describing how God is better. For example: I love to eat pizza, but *God is better still*. We don't want to suggest that God is on the same level as pizza, but this exercise can help us put our desire for God in perspective. Write at least three sentences using items from your list.

Allow students to share their list or discuss their comparisons with this new understanding. This may be a time to simply stop and have a time of prayer and worship, declaring together with your students the majesty and glory of God.

Have a time of prayer in which students simply praise God for His wonders. Encourage them not to ask God for anything during this time but only to praise Him for His blessings and majesty. Allow the Holy Spirit to lead in the duration and intensity of this time.

Once students grasp the idea of the glory of God, transition into the idea that being allowed to have access to Him is a gift. Some students may believe they come into the presence of God because they worship or sing correctly or at the right pitch. But the truth behind entering the presence of God is that it happens only because of Jesus.

ONLY BECAUSE OF THE CROSS

Here's the key: We cannot enter into the incredible presence of God *because we worship;* rather, we're allowed in *because of the work Christ did on the cross.* In other words, singing to God and raising our hands will not bring us into God's presence. Rather, being in God's presence is a gift. We move closer to the most incredible being alive because of the Cross. When we truly understand that, our worship takes on an honest, real and true perspective. Think of a worship song that talks about the importance of the Cross. Ask yourself, *What do you really know about the Cross?* Take the quiz in the Action section.

Action

For each statement below, mark whether you agree or disagree. Be prepared to give a reason why you checked what you did.

1. God has never sinned.
   Agree ☐   Disagree ☐

2. God hates sin, and sin can't be near Him.
   Agree ☐   Disagree ☐

3. A few people have never sinned, like Mother Teresa, Gandhi or Billy Graham.
   Agree ☐   Disagree ☐

4. If you're sincere about what you believe and do good stuff, you'll go to heaven.
   Agree ☐   Disagree ☐

5. Jesus Christ only made a couple of mistakes.
   Agree ☐   Disagree ☐

6. Jesus' death paid for the sins of the world.
   Agree ☐   Disagree ☐

7. God invites everyone to turn to Him in faith.
   Agree ☐   Disagree ☐

Notice the survey is not set up as a true/false quiz but as an agree/disagree survey. You may have students coming from atheistic, agnostic or universalistic perspectives and holding different beliefs. Equally, you may have students who have no idea what they believe about the Cross. At this point the idea is not to start a debate but to encourage discussion through exploration. Later in the study, specific Scripture verses will address the questions raised in the survey.

What does the Bible say about the Cross? Well, to truly understand the Cross and how it relates to our times of worship, we need to know a few things about the character of God, the work of Christ and what God asks us to do. Take a few moments to look up the following verses. Match each verse on the left to the statement on the right that best corresponds to it by drawing a line between the two.

The verse side is set up sequentially to lead a person through the plan of salvation. You may want to spend some time with each verse, explaining with your students what each passage means. Answers: (1) h, (2) f, (3) b, (4) e, (5) a, (6) c, (7) d, (8) g.

1. People who believe in Christ are saved.
2. Jesus Christ lived a sinless life.
3. Sinners can't be in God's presence.
4. You can't be saved just because you're good.
5. God is holy. He's never made a mistake.
6. Everybody sins, even your pastor.
7. The effect of sin is separation from God.
8. Jesus became the sacrifice for our sins.

a. 1 Samuel 2:2
b. Psalm 1:5
c. Romans 3:23
d. Romans 6:23
e. Ephesians 2:8-9
f. Hebrews 4:14-15
g. 2 Corinthians 5:21
h. John 3:16

As before, allow students to discuss their Break It Down answers and the following questions in small groups of two or three.

Take five minutes to share your answers with your group, and then discuss the following questions. If you're alone, find a friend or relative to discuss your thoughts with.

- Read this statement again: We are not allowed into the presence of God *because we worship*; rather, we're allowed in *because of the work Christ did on the cross*. What does this statement mean to you?
- Why do people call Jesus' death on the cross a gift? What exactly did He do for us on the cross?
- Why is it important that we understand what Jesus did for us on the cross?

≋ project revolution

Write down your ideas for community-service projects that you can complete outside the church walls. Choose one project that you or your group will put into action over the next week. This suggestion will help get you thinking about your project.

SERVANT MINDED

Pick an individual or a group that you can legitimately give some kind of gift to this week. You can do this with your group or by yourself. Perhaps you can do yard work or slip $20 in an envelope and pass it to someone on the street who might need it. Give the gift as a symbolic remembrance of the work Christ did for you on the cross. If possible, give the gift anonymously to someone who truly needs it.

≋ momentum

Promoting daily devotionals for further study can be one way of encouraging regular Scripture reading for your students. Remember to talk about the resources on the Soul Survivor Encounter website.

If you want to go further in your study of worship, you can start by looking up Scripture.

TIME IN THE WORD

Read the following passages this week. Respond to what you read in the spaces provided.

Day 1—1 Samuel 6:6
Day 2—1 Peter 1:16
Day 3—Revelation 17:14
Day 4—Philemon 2:9-11
Day 5—1 John 3:5

coming to a close

1. Have the group come back together for prayer. Choose the form of prayer that has worked the most effectively throughout the study so far.
2. You may want to soften the lights and light a candle before you move into prayer.
3. Be sensitive to students who might be having a particularly difficult week. Pray for God to give you wisdom and sensitivity in dealing with the group.

AFTER THE MEETING
1. **Evaluate**
2. **Encourage**
3. **Equip**
4. **Pray**
5. **Project Revolution**

Note: All leader's options and tips are in shaded areas.

before everyone shows up

1. Pray for all the students who will be attending and for friends they may invite.
2. Complete your own Project Revolution commitment from last week.
3. Work through the entire session on your own and mark the areas that you would like to spend more time on during the study.
4. Keep your eyes and ears open during the week for relevant celebrity quotations or news stories that demonstrate an expression of worship.
5. Gather materials for the study and make sure that all the technology that you will be using, such as a VCR or DVD player, works. Arrange seating so that everyone can see the screen or monitor.
6. View the corresponding Soul Survivor video segment ahead of time.
7. Play music and set out food to create a welcoming atmosphere.

GETTING STARTED

1. Have each small group talk about what they did this past week for their Project Revolution. Allow them to describe what happened.
2. Pray for God's guidance and grace as you begin the study.

Icebreakers

Option 1: You may want to prepare slips of paper with Bible references to be read during the meeting. When students arrive hand out the passages to be read. Be aware of students who may not like to read out loud.

Option 2: Radical Cheerleading. Divide group into two to three teams and instruct each team to come up with a cause and to create a cheer for that cause. Depending on your group, you may want to preselect the causes they cheer for and have each group choose a cause out of a hat. Their causes can be light in tone, such as a lower driving age or more sugar in soda. A cause can be serious, such as ending famines. Finally, have students perform their cheers in front of the entire group.

WHAT PEOPLE ARE SAYING

AVRIL LAVIGNE, SINGER

"My mom wouldn't even let me sing [the country song] 'Strawberry Wine,' because it said 'wine' in it and I was this little kid. She protected my image. And that's not the only reason why I don't dance around onstage, but it definitely has something to do with being brought up with tons of morals. And I'm not saying I'll never write a song with a curse word . . . but then I think about my mom, and how it would probably hurt her. So I just say 'frig' instead."[1]

SCOTT STAPP, LEAD SINGER, CREED

"I know that I believe in God and I speak with Him every day and I have a relationship with Him and I feel like He speaks with me and I feel like He's instrumental in everything that I do."[2]

DAVID BOWIE, MUSICIAN

"*Heathen* (Bowie's latest album) possibly sounds like a conversation between two people, which it kind of is—except that the other person is life or God, if there is such a higher intelligence."[3]

EMINEM, HIP-HOP ARTIST

"That's how it is with every song I do; it's therapy and it's releasing everything onto a record instead of doing any of it. I really dumped my feelings out in that song. I love my little girl enough to sing to her, for one, and two, it wasn't easy what I went through last year. Divorce is the hardest thing that I've ever worked through—not that I'm bitter or anything like that. I'm a better person because I went through it, but it was hard. And at first you don't know what to do. You know, I put the blame on everything. I put the blame on myself, I put the blame on my career. But as I got through it, I stepped back and looked at the whole picture."[4]

INTERVIEW

Subject: Tim Hughes, musician, worship leader
Tim Hughes wrote the songs "Light of the World," "Beautiful One" and "Name Above All Names."
Soul Survivor: How do you know God is real in your life?
Tim Hughes: God has revealed Himself to me in so many ways that I know He's real. Throughout my life as I've chosen to trust in God, I've seen that He's faithful. He's always been faithful. I remember one time when I was 19. I went to South Africa for a year with a friend. After a couple of weeks, my friend got sick and had to return home. I was left feeling very alone and very scared. In that place I turned to God and prayed like mad. He was so faithful. What could have been a disaster ended up being one of the most special years of my life. When you experience God's continual faithfulness you know He's real.

See the rest of this interview and more thought-provoking quotes at www.SoulSurvivorEncounter.com.

video segment

Show the corresponding Soul Survivor video clip from the *Real Life & Undignified Worship DVD*. Before students watch the video, hand out pieces of paper and pens or pencils. Ask them to write down what they feel as they watch the clip.

≡ *the story*

Summarize the concepts presented in this section, or have students alternate reading each section.

RADICAL CHEERLEADING

Teenaged and 20-something activists around the world have turned an American tradition into political theater. It's a new movement called Radical Cheerleading, and squads have been reported worldwide. Instead of cheering for a sports team, radical cheerleaders express their support for causes like protesting abortion or war, fighting racism or opposing various economic policies. Radical cheerleaders gather where they think they need to be heard—on street corners, in parks, outside rock concerts or on college campuses.[5]

Sadly, discussing expressions of worshiping God can be divisive within the Body of Christ. Different group members may prefer different expressions of worship based on the traditions they have encountered. The point of this lesson is not to begin a debate about the merits of various worship styles but rather to allow students to develop convictions based on scriptural principles.

RADICAL EXPRESSION

How do people express what they feel passionately about? Think about the radical cheerleaders you just read about. How do you express what you believe? Have you ever felt something so deeply, so passionately that you just had to do something about it?

Maybe there was a time when you felt very angry and you went for a run—sports can be a great way to express or release strong feelings. Maybe you saw the autumn leaves falling in such a way that you captured the moment by snapping a picture—photography is another means of expression.

TREE TRUNK OF WORSHIP

How do you express worship to God? When you encounter God and all His amazing glory, how do you thank God for His infinite worth?

Luckily, Scripture doesn't limit us to just one method. On the contrary, Scripture shows us how worshiping God encompasses a variety of expressions including singing, dancing, speech, playing an instrument, shouting, whispering, praying, listening, serving or even being silent. Our creative God made us in His own image. He invites us to reflect His creativity in our expressions of worship.

The Bible points to at least four foundational principles to keep in mind when worshiping God. Think of the principles as pieces of a tree trunk from which various branches and leaves spring forth. The branches and leaves are the actual expressions of worship.

Read each tree trunk piece and the Scripture references that make up the foundational principles of worship and complete each Action item.

This idea is based around four key convictions regarding foundational principles: Worship is intimate, reverent and true, and it strengthens the church. Of course, this is not an exhaustive list. If you or the tradition you represent believes strongly in a certain direction, feel free to add another foundational conviction from Scripture or reword a conviction a

different way. You could mention that worship is commanded throughout Scripture (see Revelation 19:10). In other words, it's not an option for believers not to worship God.

1. **Tree Trunk Piece:** Expressions of worship are *intimate* (see Galatians 4:6-7). Christ's work enables you to become a child of God. If you believe, God is your father and you are His son or daughter. Through His Holy Spirit you can enjoy closeness with God. Because of that closeness you can call Him *Abba*—the Aramaic word for "daddy"—the word a little child would use when addressing the father he or she loves.

Action

What do you think? Because of the Holy Spirit you can be close to God. Will that thought affect how you worship Him? Is it important to find intimacy with God when you worship Him?

2. **Tree Trunk Piece:** Expressions of worship must be *reverent* because God is worthy (see 1 Chronicles 16:25). God is the King of kings and Lord of lords. You shouldn't act superficial, flippant or disrespectful toward Him. Exodus 19 describes God as so holy that His people had to prepare physically and spiritually to worship Him. His people must approach Him with the utmost respect, adoration and awe for both His power and His love.

Action

Read Exodus 19:16-22 and Malachi 1:14. Will your attitude of reverence before God affect how you worship Him? How do these verses give you insight into the radical holiness of God?

3. **Tree Trunk Piece:** Expressions of worship must be *true* (see John 4:24). True worship *happens* in our spirit—in the center of our will. One's behavior merely *expresses* worship. This means that when you sing, the singing itself is not worship to God; singing simply expresses the worship you feel in your heart. True worship happens in the attitude of the hearts as you sing, dance or serve.

Action

Read John 4:22-24. How does your knowledge of worshiping God in spirit and truth affect how you worship Him? Can you fake worship if true worship can only happen in your heart?

4. **Tree Trunk Piece:** Expressions of worship must *strengthen* the Church (see 1 Corinthians 14:26). Scripture indicates that expressions of worship must strengthen believers, not tear them apart. If an expression of worship causes people to disagree, ask yourself why. Some expressions used for worship could be morally wrong or require you to do things Scripture prohibits. Some types of worship may be appropriate for one culture, type of personality or generation of people, but not another. That's okay. Worshiping God in different ways is not wrong or dishonest as long as the expression agrees with the Bible.

Action

Read 1 Corinthians 14:26 and answer the following questions: If worship strengthens the Church and unifies believers, does that mean we can only play music that everyone enjoys? How can worship strengthen the Church if people disagree on the kind of music used?

Spend time briefly reviewing the four foundational principles.

☰ break it down

According to Scripture, worship must be *intimate*, *reverent*, *true* and an expression that *strengthens* the Church. These four qualities exist as the trunk of the worship tree. The specific expressions of worship act as the branches and the leaves of the tree. Scripture also indicates that as long as these principles are in order, various expressions will change depending on seasons and situations.

Action

What else does Scripture say about the branches and the leaves? Read about the following biblical expressions of worship, and then complete the first five expressions of worship to match the last seven listed:

Exodus 3:5—
Psalm 40:6-8—
Psalm 47:1—
Psalm 149:3—

Psalm 150:3-5—Worship by musical instruments and dance
Isaiah 66:23; Ephesians 3:14—Worship by bowing and kneeling
Ephesians 5:19; Psalm 40:3—Worship through song and hymns
1 Thessalonians 5:18—Worship by thanksgiving
1 Timothy 2:8; Psalm 63:4—Worship by lifting hands
Hebrews 13:15-16—Worship of praise and sharing with others
Revelation 5:8-9—Worship through prayer, incense and song

Your tradition may not permit using instruments as worship, and worshiping God by removing shoes may not be commonly practiced, although it is found in Scripture. Rather than expound on each expression, the point of this section is to show that a variety of biblical expressions of worship exist. Scripture allows worshipers to approach God in a variety of creative means.

☰ comeback

Allow students to discuss the answers in small groups of two or three.

Take about five minutes to discuss the following questions with your group. If you're alone, find a friend or relative with whom you can discuss what you're thinking.

- Intimacy and reverence are two of the foundational principles in the tree trunk. How can a person be both intimate with and reverent toward God?
- Do you think there's ever a conflict between the two?
- How does your knowledge of God's creativity help you express your worship to Him?

The point is that God is a creative God. He made us creative people. Worshiping Him in creative ways can involve a wide range of the arts, including sculpture, music, film, dance, photography, literature, painting and drawing.

⚡ project revolution

Write down your ideas for a community-service project that you can complete outside your church walls. Choose one that you or your group will put into action this week. The suggestions in this section should help you think about your project.

UNCOMMON WORSHIP

This week, get together with your group and have a worship time at somebody's house. During the worship time, utilize expressions of worship that are uncommon to you. You might want to play instruments you don't know how to play, dance, pray or burn incense. You could stage a worship night where painting is the only available form of worship expression. Gather large pieces of paper, brushes and paints, and then let your group declare the glory of God through their art. You might want to play worship music softly in the background.

VIDEO WORSHIP

Grab a video camera and create a worship movie. Instead of writing a worship song in which music declares the greatness of God, make a home video that does the same thing. What could you shoot on video to show God at work? What could you take pictures of that display God's attributes? You may want to interview people on the video, shoot nature scenes or show people conducting acts of service. Get creative, but keep it short. Shoot the videos one day, and then show them to the group the next time you meet.
Option: Create a worship collage or gallery of worship photos from pictures you took.

⚡ momentum

Promoting Scripture references for further study can be one way of encouraging daily Scripture reading for students. In fact, remind students that spending time in God's Word is an act of worship in itself.

Go further by reading the suggested selections from the Bible this week.

TIME IN THE WORD

Read the following passages this week as part of your time with God. In the space provided, write your thoughts about what you read.

Day 1—Psalms 149:3
Day 2—Matthew 6:9-13
Day 3—Nehemiah1:4-6
Day 4—1 Samuel 1:1-10
Day 5—Psalm 5

coming to a close

1. Have the group come back together for prayer. Again, they can either pray with a partner or pray together with the whole group. Be sure to have index cards available for students to write down their prayer requests and then pass around to the others.
2. Remind students that if anyone wants to talk further about a relationship with Jesus Christ that you would love to talk with him or her.

AFTER THE MEETING

1. **Evaluate**
2. **Encourage**
3. **Equip**
4. **Pray**
5. **Project Revolution**

Note: All leader's options and tips are in shaded areas.

before everyone shows up

1. Pray for the students who will attend and for friends they may invite.
2. Complete your own Project Revolution commitment from last week.
3. Work through the entire session on your own ahead of time and mark the different areas in which you would like to spend more time during the study. As you prepare, ask God to give you creativity and a heart to listen.
4. Keep your eyes and ears open during the week for relevant celebrity quotations or news stories that demonstrate ideas of worship and heaven.
5. Gather materials for the study and make sure that all the technology that you will be using, such as a VCR or DVD player, works. Arrange seating so that everyone can see the screen or monitor.
6. View the corresponding Soul Survivor video segment ahead of time.
7. Play music and set out food to create a welcoming atmosphere.

GETTING STARTED

1. When everyone has arrived, ask students to partner up with someone they haven't met or don't know very well. Instruct them to answer this question: What do you think heaven will be like? Have them briefly share their partner's answer with the group.
2. Let each small group share what they did this past week for their Project Revolution and what happened.
3. Pray for God's guidance and grace as you begin the study.

Icebreakers

You may want to prepare slips of paper with Bible references to be read during the meeting. When students arrive, hand out the passages to be read. Be aware of students who may not like to read out loud.

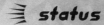

WHAT PEOPLE ARE SAYING

DAVE MATTHEWS, MUSICIAN

Dave Matthews discussing his new song, "Bartender": "It's not the happiest idea in the world, thinking about dying and what your life means. And the Jesus thing is an impossible comparison: Can God come out of the sky, take the form of this bartender in front of me and save my life?"[1]

BILLY CORGAN, MUSICIAN

"Faith is the great energy—as long as one has faith, you're willing to try, to take another chance. I don't think God really cares how you do it, just that you're willing to do it. This is not ice-skating. God wants you to amble toward the right spot on the horizon. You might [screw up] but the idea is that you're willing to get up and keep moving toward that light."[2]

OSWALD CHAMBERS, AUTHOR

"Continually examine your attitude toward God to see if you are willing to 'go out' in every area of your life, trusting God entirely. It is this attitude that keeps you in constant wonder, because you don't know what God is going to do next."[3]

INTERVIEW

Subject: David Ruis, worship leader, speaker

Soul Survivor: How do you define "worship?" What does that word mean to you?

David Ruis: To me the concept of worship takes on a whole breadth of unique meaning for those who embrace Christ. He becomes the focus of worship that is both intimate and filled with awe. It fills our whole life's experience, because He is not just a distant ruler who deserves worship (even demons recognize this; James says they believe and they tremble), but He has become Emmanuel and actually dwells with us and in us. So my heart sings and He becomes the center of that song. My perspectives and values change, and He is at the center of that transformation and lifestyle. My whole world revolves around Him—but beyond the simplicity of

a pop song lyric—He truly has become my love and obsession so that even if I just simply "eat and drink," it's all done to His glory. Not because of liturgy, but because He is my life, my hope—my everything.

See the rest of this interview and more thought-provoking quotes at www.SoulSurvivorEncounter.com.

OOPS

Canadian rock singer Alanis Morissette recently finished a show in front of 14,000 screaming fans by shouting: "Thank you, Brazil!"

There was one problem. She was at Monumental Stadium—in *Peru.*

Some Peruvian newspapers criticized her, while others said her outstanding performance made up for it. The newspaper *Ojo* said, "We have already forgiven her thanks to her magical performance in which we witnessed a true rock star. It was the first time something like that happened over here, but it must have been the emotion she felt for being in Peru."[5]

Like Alanis Morrisette, have you ever reached the end of something only to have it turn out different from what you had imagined? Have you ever reached a goal or destination only to mess it up a little bit or face disappointment?

Action

Write down some thoughts about your future. Ask yourself four questions and answer them in the space provided.

1. What do I look forward to?
2. What will happen when my goal is reached?

3. How would I respond if I discover that reaching my goal isn't what I imagined it to be?
4. What if it is all I imagined it to be and more?

FUTURE GLORY

Scripture paints a clear picture of what the future will be for followers of Jesus Christ. According to the Bible, believers will spend all eternity in the presence of God. Life will be an incredible, never-ending worship session.

Maybe that sounds fantastic to you, and now you've got a clear picture of what it's like in the presence of God. Maybe you're thinking, *Yeah, spending time with God for all eternity will be great, but there are sure some things I want to do first here on Earth.* Don't worry if that's how you feel—it seems logical when lots of life stretches out before you. It's natural to look forward to earthly goals.

At the same time, Scripture challenges us to look forward to heavenly goals above everything else. If you feel hesitant about a future of worshiping God, perhaps it's because you're seeing the future from an earthly perspective, not a heavenly one.

Imagine this for a moment. You are standing next to Jesus in heaven, looking down at Earth. An incredible party swirls around you and no words will do it justice. Your definition of "cool" on Earth falls far short of what you are actually experiencing in God's presence. Heaven is better than a driver's license, better than graduating, better than all the amazing delights that go along with being in love.

As you stand there, Jesus looks at a friend of yours on Earth and extends an invitation. Christ says, "Come on up. You're invited. Join the party." Your friend looks at Christ and says, "Nah, actually, I'd rather have a new pickup truck."

The point is not to chastise students if they honestly long for things on Earth but to challenge their concepts and show them how much better an eternity with God will be than anything they can imagine. When the study talks about worshiping God for all eternity, some students may still imagine this to mean a really long time to sing, which they may or may not enjoy. By this point in the study, students' concepts of worshiping God should have broadened to include aspects of an all-encompassing activity and lifestyle. But it may be prudent at this point to review some definitions of worship, particularly in light of an eternal perspective.

Action

What would you say to your friend? How would you convince him that being in heaven with Jesus is amazing? Take a moment and write down your thoughts in the space provided. If you feel like it, draw a rough sketch of your reaction or discussion.

Scripture describes a similar situation in Romans 8:18-21. According to this passage, being with God is an amazing time of worship, but it takes an unearthly perspective to put that in view.

Have you seen anyone go through a tough time and say, "I don't know why I have to experience this. I didn't ask to be born in the first place. Why me?" Sometimes people feel as though life isn't fair, and it is true that no one chose to be born into a sinful world. But what else isn't fair? Adam's choice to sin wasn't fair to God.

God allowed Adam's choice as part of His plan to allow people to experience salvation and share in God's eternal glory. Have you ever thought that God didn't have to allow people to share in the greatness of a future with Him? God didn't have to share at all. So while it may not be fair that we have to deal with frustrations on Earth, it's equally unfair that we have the incredible privilege of sharing in His glory.

Use caution—Do not rush this part of the lesson.

It's valid for people of all ages to sense injustice that Adam made a choice that negatively affected everyone (see Romans 5:12). Yet the good news is that God allowed Adam's choice as one element of His perfect plan of salvation.

And the reality is that salvation is a gift that no person deserves. Who are we to warrant so great a gift? What's not fair about salvation is that we benefited from the Cross even though we did nothing for it. God gave us salvation only because of His marvelous love.

When students grasp the unfairness of the gospel, it can put the unfairness of being born into depravity into a whole new perspective: I was born into sin (bummer), but I'm also invited to experience God's glory (how amazing).

Action

Read Romans 8:18-21. Think through what it says and write down your reaction. These verses say that all of creation experiences hardship. How have you seen this happen in your own life or in the world around you?

Why do you think God gives us such an amazing gift, allowing us to share eternity with Him?

 break it down

WORSHIP AND ETERNITY

Unlike Alanis Morissette in Peru, followers of Christ know there are no mistakes in their future. What does a future enjoying God's presence and worshiping Him actually look like? We see a glimpse of it in the Bible.

Different gatherings of believers interpret end times in different ways. The main point here is to create a strong desire in the students to live for God. You may have students in your group who react strongly to statement 6, particularly if they are currently experiencing a season of deep sorrow. You may want to slow the group down and spend time praying together.

Action

Let's test your ideas about what a future with God in heaven will be like. Write the appropriate letter beside each statement.

- Write **S** for **Scripture**—This is a statement from Scripture that is true.
- Write **P** for **Perhaps**—This may or may not be true. We don't know.
- Write **NW** for **No Way**—This is completely untrue.

(Check your answers at the end of the session)

1. Heaven is an incredible city, as high as it is long as it is wide. _____
2. We'll be able to fly and jump unheard-of distances. _____
3. There won't be any sun or moon. _____
4. No one will face any judgment according to what he or she did in life. _____
5. We'll sit around on clouds feeling bored all day. _____
6. There will be no tears, death, mourning, crying or pain. _____
7. God will dwell with humankind and we'll worship God forever. _____
8. There will be spectacular food to eat. _____
9. The surfing, sailing, water skiing and swimming will be excellent. _____
10. If I don't get married here on Earth, I'll get married in heaven. _____

 comeback

As usual, allow students to discuss the Break It Down answers in small groups, after which they can tackle the Comeback questions.

Take about five minutes to discuss the following questions with your group. If you are alone, find a friend, parent, pastor or someone else close to you with whom you can discuss what you're thinking.

- What do you look forward to on Earth and why?
- Why do people look forward to earthly things more than to eternity with God?
- When you view your salvation as an undeserved gift, how could that affect the way you worship God?

Encourage adult leaders to answer the first question and to set the tone for how deep the students' answers will or will not go.

 project revolution

Write down your ideas for research or service projects that you can do this week. Then choose a project that you or your group will put into action. The suggestions in this section will help you get started in deciding on your project.

SENIOR SURVEY

Visit a retirement home to talk to the residents there. Record the answers you get. Make sure you ask for their name, their birth date and other essential information. Ask them about their jobs, schooling, spouse and children. Finally ask these two questions: What do young people need to know about getting older? What's the most important thing in life? Have each member of your group complete at least three surveys using these questions. Share the results with your group, even though this is the last session.

VISITING CHILDREN

Get permission to visit a children's hospital. Ask the hospital supervisor how you can best cheer up the children. Maybe you can read stories to them, dress up in costumes or give out small gifts. (Make sure you get specific permission from the supervisor before you give out anything.) Maybe you could host a worship service on a Sunday morning. Find out what the needs are first; then get creative.

momentum

Promoting Scripture references can be one way of worshiping God daily.

If you want to go further, check out the Time in the Word verses.

TIME IN THE WORD

Read the following passages this week as part of your time with God. In the space provided, write down your thoughts about the verses you've just read.

Day 1—Philemon 2:9-11
Day 2—Revelation 4:2
Day 3—Revelation 14:6-7
Day 4—Philemon 1:21-26
Day 5—1 Corinthians 15:51-52

coming to a close

1. Have the group come back together for prayer. Allow each student to say a few words in prayer as you close the final session of this study.
2. Soften the lights and light a candle before you move into prayer. Allow the silence and the candle to help center the group.

AFTER THE MEETING

1. **Evaluate:** The leaders should spend time evaluating the overall effectiveness of the study. Take time to talk about how God worked, what went well, what did not go well. Take notes for the next study that you pursue as a youth group. If you want to continue this series, order the next study in the Soul Survivor Encounter. See the website www.SoulSurvivorEncounter.com for details.

2. **Encourage:** During the week contact the students (phone calls, notes of encouragement, e-mails or instant messages) and let them know you are praying for them.
3. **Equip:** Get prepared to start your next study or next group meeting.
4. **Pray:** Prayerfully prepare yourself for either the next meeting or a new study.
5. **Project Revolution:** Encourage students to continue thinking about and completing interactive projects that occur outside the walls of your church.

FINAL NOTE

You have done a tremendous task by caring for your group throughout this study. Take some time to rest and give God thanks for His goodness.

Quiz Answers
(1) **S**—see Revelation 21:1-2,10-21; (2) **P**—see 1 Corinthians 15:51-52; (3) **S**—see Revelation 21:23; 22:5; (4) **NW**—see Isaiah 66:16; (5) **NW**—see Revelation 22:3-5; (6) **S**—see Revelation 21:4; (7) **S**—see Revelation 21:3; (8) **P**—see Revelation 22:2; (9) **NW**—see Revelation 21:1-2; (10) **NW**—see Luke 20:34-35.

Session One

1. Mel Gibson, "Even the Bad Times Make You Better," interviewed by Dotson Rayder, *Parade*, (July 28, 2002), p. 1.
2. Bono, quoted in John Waters, *Race of Angels* (Belfast, Northern Ireland: The Blackstaff Press, 1994), p. 154.
3. The Dalai Lama, *The Simple Path* (Rochester, VT: Thorsons Publishers, 2000), p. 12.
4. Dan Haseltine, "Light for the Dark Continent," *Relevant*, vol. 1, issue 2, (May/June 2003), p. 36.

Session Two

1. Beyoncé Knowles, "A Date with Destiny," interview by Jancee Dunn, *Rolling Stone* (May 24, 2001). http://www.rollingstone.com/features/coverstory/featuregen.asp?pid=1787&cf=2684 (accessed February 12, 2004).
2. Steven Tyler, "Tyler Dreams On," interview by Austin Scaggs, *Rolling Stone* (July 29, 2003). http://www.rollingstone.com/news/newsarticle.asp?nid=18443&cf=18 (accessed February 12, 2004).
3. Miranda Otto, quoted in "Life Lessons from Middle-Earth," *Plugged In*, vol. 8, no. 1 (January 2003), p. 4.
4. Layne Staley, "To Hell and Back," interview by Jon Wiederhorn, *Rolling Stone* (February 8, 1996). http://rollingstone.com/news/newsarticle.asp?nid=15807&cf=19 (accessed February 12, 2004).
5. Clay Aiken, "Achin for Clay," interview by Dawn Holmgren, *Guideposts for Teens*, vol. 6, no. 2 (December/January 2004), p. 10.
6. Mike Pilavachi, *Soul Survivor* (Ventura, CA: Regal Books, 2004), p. 106.

Session Three

1. Sharon Stone, "'Really Nice to Be Alive,' Stone Says," interview by Ann Oldenberg, *USA Today*, April 22, 2002, sec. D, p. 2.
2. Paul McCartney, "People of the Year: Paul McCartney," interview by Anthony DeCurtis, *Rolling Stone* (December 6, 2001). http://www.rollingstone.com/news/newsarticle.asp?nid=15095&cf=1088 (accessed February 12, 2004).
3. Bob Dylan, "Bob Dylan: The Rolling Stone Interview," interview by Mikal Gilmore, *Rolling Stone* (November 22, 2001). http://www.rollingstone.com/features/featuregen.asp?pid=85&cf=184 (accessed February 12, 2004).
4. Afroman, quoted at Gil Kaufman, "Afroman Drops Bong for Bible," *Rolling Stone* (May 29, 2003). http://www.rollingstone.com/news/newsarticle.asp?nid=18126&cf=2043130 (accessed February 12, 2004).
5. C. S. Lewis, *Reflections on the Psalms* (Orlando, FL: Harvest Books, 1958), p. 95.
6. Mother Teresa, *No Greater Love* (Novato, CA: New World Library, 1989), p. 163.

Session Four

1. Axl Rose, quoted in "Youth Culture Update," *Youthworker* (January/February 2003), p. 14.
2. Colin Powell, quoted in "Youth Culture Update," *Youthworker* (January/February 2003), p. 14.
3. Kirsten Dunst, "Kirsten Dunst Busts Out," interview by David A. Keeps, *Rolling Stone* (May 23, 2002), p. 69.
4. Orlando Bloom, quoted inVicki Arkoff, "10 Reasons Why Orlando's Bloomin' Great," *Guideposts for Teens* (December/January 2004), p. 17
5. Cornelius Tacitus, *Annals XV, 44*, quoted in Paul McKechnie, *The First Christian Centuries: Perspectives on the Early Church* (Downers Grove, IL: Intervarsity Press, 2001), p. 60.
6. Brother Andrew, "Overcoming the Fear of Reaching Out," *Open Doors*, May 12, 2003. http://www.opendoors.org.au/pgs/artcl/ba03.htm (accessed October 5, 2003).

Session Five

1. Scott Stapp, quoted at Steven Chean, "The Need for Creed," *USA Weekend* (August 2, 2002). http://www.usaweekend.com/02_issues/020804/020804creed.html (accessed February 12, 2004).
2. Madonna, quoted in "Overheard," *Plugged In*, vol. 8, no. 7 (July 2003), p. 10.
3. Beck, quoted in Chuck Klosterman, "Bringing Beck Alive," *Spin* (July 23, 2003), p. 80.
4. Mel Gibson, quoted at Carl Limbacher, "Focus on the Family Praises Gibson's Film," *Newsmax.com* (June 29, 2003). http://www.newsmax.com/showinside.shtml?a=2003/6/29/230135 (accessed February 5, 2004).
5. Tom Yorke, quoted at Chuck Klosterman, "Fitter Happier: Radiohead Return," *Spin* (June 29, 2003). http://www.spin-magazine.com/modules.php?op=modload&name=News&file=article&sid=80 (accessed February 12, 2004).
6. Dave Havok, quoted at Kate Stroup, "Despairing with AFI," *Rolling Stone* (March 25, 2003). http://www.rollingstone.com/features/featuregen.asp?pid=1606&cf=6201 (accessed February 12, 2004).

Session Six

1. Jason Wade, quoted in "Overheard," *Plugged In*, vol. 8, no. 2 (February 2003), p. 10.
2. Alicia Keyes, "To Be Alicia Keys: Young, Gifted and in Control," interview by John Pareles, *New York Times*, January 27, 2002, sec. 2, p. 1.
3. Shakira, "Shakira," interview by Evan Wright, *Rolling Stone* (April 11, 2002), p. 72.
4. Friedrich Nietzsche, *Beyond Good and Evil* (New York: Random House, 1966), p. 101.
5. Dave Grohl, quoted at Alex Pappedemas, "Foo Fighters," *Spin* (July 23, 2003). http://www.spinmagazine.com/modules.php?op=modload&name=News&file=article&sid=159 (accessed February 12, 2004).
6. Eusebius, *History of the Church*, (London: Penguin Group, 1990), p. 35.

Session Seven

1. Kelly Osborn, "Kelly Osborn Says," interview by Sarah Lewitinn, *Spin* (April 2002), p. 74.
2. Nicole Kidman, quoted in Ann Oldenburg, "Nicole's Hour," *USA Today*, March 7, 2003, sec. D, p. 8.
3. Mike Shinoda, quoted at Alex Pappademas, "Rock 101: Linkin Park," *Spin* (July 8, 2003). http://www.spinmagazine.com/modules.php?op=modload&name=News&file=article&sid=90 (accessed February 12, 2004).
4. Sonny Sandoval, "Sonny Sandoval of P.O.D.," interview by Don Zulaica, *Livedaily.com*, December 24, 2003. http://www.livedaily.com/news/5929.html (accessed February 6, 2004).

Session Eight

1. Bono, quoted at David Fricke, "U2 Finds What It's Looking For," *Rolling Stone* (October 1, 1992). http://www.rollingstone.com/features/featuregen.asp?pid=1989&cf=45 (accessed February 13, 2004).
2. Zachary Levi, quoted in Dan Ewald, "Zachary Levi," *Christian Single* (February 2004), p. 12.
3. Sean Combs, quoted in Mikal Gilmore, "Puff Daddy," *Rolling Stone* (August 7, 1997), p. 52.
4. Alex Field, "Beyoncé Knowles: Dangerously Spiritual," *Relevant* (July/August 2003), p. 50.
5. Curtis Kuhn, "Book Review: The Unquenchable Worshipper," *Worship Leader* (March/April, 2002). Used with permission.

Session Nine

1. Leah Furman and Elina Furman, *Heart and Soul: The Lauryn Hill Story* (New York: Ballantine Books, 1999), p. 58.
2. Lenny Kravitz, "Interview with Lenny Kravitz," interview by Davin Seay, *LennyKravitz.com*. www.lennykravitz.com/extras/interviews (accessed February 13, 2004).
3. Sean "P. Diddy" Combs, interview by Sway Calloway, *MTV News*.
4. Tom Petty, quoted in David Wild, "Tom Petty Is Pissed," *Rolling Stone* (October 23, 2002), p. 34.
5. Associated Press, "Fatal Prank Sends Jolt Through Amish Community," *The Columbian*, September 7, 2003, sec. A, p. 1.
6. *Merriam-Webster's Collegiate Dictionary*, 11th ed., s.v. "response."

Session Ten

1. Mary J. Blige, "Cover Story: Mary J. Blige," interview by Jancee Dunn, *Rolling Stone* (October 31, 2002), p. 62.
2. Johnny Cash, "Johnny Cash: The Spirit Is Willing," interview by Patrick Carr, *Journal of Country Music*, vol. 22, no. 3 (April 14, 2002). http://www.cmt.com/artists/news /1455988/07092002/cash_johnny.jhtml (accessed February 13, 2004).
3. Alan Jackson, "Alan Jackson," interview by Alanna Nash, *USA Weekend* (November 3, 2002). http://www.usaweekend.com/02_issues/021103/021103alan_jac kson.html (accessed February 13, 2004).
4. Bob Dylan, "Bob Dylan: The Rolling Stone Interview," interview by Kurt Loder, *Rolling Stone* (June 21, 1984). http://www.rolling-stone.com/features/coverstory/featuregen.asp?pid =2006&cf=184 (accessed February 13, 2004).

Session Eleven

1. Avril Lavigne, "Cover Story: Avril Lavigne," interview by Jenny Eliscu, *Rolling Stone* (March 20, 2003).

http://www.rollingstone.com/features/featuregen.asp?pid=1555 &cf=2044243 (accessed February 13, 2004).
2. Scott Stapp, "MXTV Creed Interview," interview by Tim Bisagno and Chris Seay, *MXTV Mission X*. http://www.missionx.org/mxtv/mxtv.htm (accessed February 13, 2004).
3. David Bowie, quoted in Elysa Gardner, "Bowie Has Faith in Heathen," *USA Today*, June 11, 2002, sec. D, p. 10.
4. Eminem, "Eminem: The Rolling Stone Interview," interview by Anthony Bozza, *Rolling Stone* (July 4, 2002). http://www.rolling stone.com/features/featuregen.asp?pid=754 (accessed February 13, 2004).
5. Barbara Kantrowitz, Karen Springen and Jenny Hontz, "We're Here, We Cheer, Get Used to It," *Newsweek* (September 29, 2003). http://www.msnbc.msn.com/id/3668484/ (accessed February 13, 2004).

Session Twelve

1. Dave Matthews, "Back in the Groove: Dave Matthews Band," interview by Dave Fricke, *Rolling Stone* (August 8, 2002). http://www.rollingstone.com/features/coverstory/ featuregen.asp?pid=938&cf=2047370 (accessed February 13, 2004).
2. Billy Corgan, "Born Again Corgan," interview by David Fricke, *Rolling Stone* (March 12, 2003). http://www.rollingstone.com/features/featuregen.asp?pid=1592 &cf=2045135 (accessed February 13, 2004).
3. Oswald Chambers, *My Utmost for His Highest: An Updated Edition in Today's Language* (Grand Rapids, MI: Discovery House, 1992), p. 4.
4. "Alanis Makes Brazil Gaffe in Peru," *BBC News* (September 24, 2003). http://news.bbc.co.uk/2/hi/entertainment/3136342.stm (accessed February 9, 2004).

A REVOLUTIONARY APPROACH TO YOUTH MINISTRY!

The **Soul Survivor Encounter Kit** includes five *Real Life & Undignified Worship Student Magazines,* one *Real Life & Undignified Worship Leader's Guide,* one *Real Life & Undignified Worship DVD,* one *Soul Survivor Guide to Youth Ministry,* one *Soul Survivor Prayer Ministry* and one *Soul Survivor Guide to Service Projects.*
ISBN 08307.35267

Soul Survivor is a dynamic British youth ministry that has impacted hundreds of thousands of young people worldwide through its powerful youth events for over 10 years. Soul Survivor has released such leaders as **Matt and Beth Redman** and **Tim Hughes**. With **Soul Survivor Encounter**, youth leaders around the world can use the successful elements of the Soul Survivor ministry to create in their young people a passionate commitment to worshiping God and to putting their faith into action.

The kit's relevant resources include contemporary student magazines with 12 interactive sessions, as well as leadership materials, intense DVD segments and a website. Sessions feature interviews with leaders, artists and young people; quotations from pop culture; activities; devotional verses; Scripture discussions and interactive activities.

Soul Survivor Encounter gives youth leaders a radically **new** and **proven** way to reach young people for Christ. This biblical and relevant program is sure to ignite a revolution in youth ministry that will impact generations to come. Be a part of it!

Available at your local Christian bookstore
www.SoulSurvivorEncounter.com

SOUL SURVIVOR LEADERSHIP RESOURCES

Soul Survivor Guide to Youth Ministry

This manual details the history of the Soul Survivor ministry and presents a vision for raising up young leaders. Includes methods for developing leadership abilities, the 10 most common mistakes leaders make and guidelines for mentoring young leaders—a great resource for youth groups, study groups, pastors and aspiring young leaders.

ISBN 08307.35305

Soul Survivor Guide to Service Projects

This guide explains an important aspect of the Soul Survivor ministry: action evangelism or communicating the gospel through service, justice and love. Packed with ideas for service projects, examples of action evangelism, tips for youth leaders and methods of outreach and follow-up, this inspiring manual will help youth leaders galvanize young Christians to reach out to their community and make a difference!

ISBN 08307.35291

Soul Survivor Prayer Ministry How to Pray for Others

This handy pocket-sized book explains how you can establish an effective prayer ministry. The book features prayer guidelines including how to pray for forgiveness, how to pray about making a decision for Christ and how to pray for others. These simple guidelines will ignite a powerful prayer ministry in your church!

ISBN 08307.35275

BREAKTHROUGH BOOKS FROM SOUL SURVIVOR

Soul Survivor
Finding Passion and Purpose in the Dry Places
Mike Pilavachi

Mike Pilavachi, leader and founder of the Soul Survivor youth movement, has touched and inspired thousands with his message that the desert is ultimately a place we should desire to be. Only when we come to the end of ourselves and our desire for independence can we come to the beginning of God.

ISBN 08307.33248

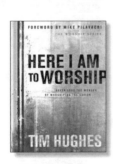

Here I Am to Worship
Never Lose the Wonder of Worshiping the Savior
Tim Hughes

Dove Award-winning songwriter Tim Hughes gives you practical and spiritual guidance for worship—from songwriting to having the right heart attitude in praising our Father. God wants to take you deeper but only when you proclaim, "Here I am to worship!"

ISBN 08307.33221

Soul Sister
The Truth About Being God's Girl
Beth Redman

This book is for soul sisters everywhere—a generation of girls living to please the heart of God. Beth Redman walks us through many of life's difficult issues and shows us how important it is to get into God's Word and to get God's Word into us.

ISBN 08307.32128

The Unquenchable Worshipper
Coming Back to the Heart of Worship
Matt Redman

Matt Redman writes to a certain kind of worshipper. Unquenchable. Unstoppable. Undignified. Undone. For everyone who wants to learn how to worship—this is an unbelievable, unsurpassed and uncharted experience!

ISBN 08307.29135

The Heart of Worship Files
Featuring Contributions from Some of Today's Most Experienced Lead Worshippers
Compiled by *Matt Redman*

A book for all of those who find themselves on a pilgrimage of passionate worship. Includes contributions from Louie Giglio, Tim Hughes, Graham Kendrick, Martyn Layzell, Chris Tomlin, Don Williams, Darlene Zschech and many more.

ISBN 08307.32616

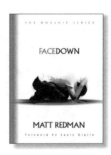

Facedown
Matt Redman

When you face up to God's glory, you find yourself facedown in worship. God wants us to be more than aware of His presence. He calls us to be awestruck by it. How do we reach this state? By totally surrendering to God through worship!

ISBN 08307.32462

Available at your local Christian bookstore
www.SoulSurvivorEncounter.com